All About
C·I·T·R·U·S
& Subtropical Fruits

Created and designed by
the editorial staff of
ORTHO Books

Project Manager	**Ernie Tasaki**
Project Editor	**Rick Bond**
Contributing Editor	**Lance Walheim**
Writers	**Maggie Klein** **Paul Moore** **Claude Sweet**
Designer	**Ron Hildebrand**
Major Photographer	**Pam Peirce**
Illustrators	**Ron Hildebrand** **Ronda Hildebrand**

Ortho Books

Publisher
Robert L. Iacopi

Editorial Director
Min S. Yee

Managing Editors
Jim Beley
Anne Coolman
Susan Lammers
Michael D. Smith
Sally W. Smith

Production Director
Ernie S. Tasaki

Editors
Richard H. Bond
Alice E. Mace

System Manager
Christopher Banks

System Consultant
Mark Zielinski

Asst. System Managers
Linda Bouchard
William F. Yusavage

Photographic Director
Alan Copeland

Photographers
Laurie A. Black
Richard A. Christman

Asst. Production Manager
Darcie S. Furlan

Associate Editor
Jill Fox

Production Editors
Deborah Cowder
Don Mosley
Anne Pederson

Chief Copy Editor
Rebecca Pepper

Photo Editors
Kate O'Keeffe
Pam Peirce
Raymond F. Quinton

National Sales Manager
Charles H. Aydelotte

Sales Associate
Susan B. Boyle

Operations Assistant
Gail L. Davis

Administrative Assistant
Georgiann Wright

Address all inquiries to
Ortho Books
Chevron Chemical Company
Consumer Products Division
575 Market Street
San Francisco, CA 94105

ACKNOWLEDGMENTS

Subtropical fruit recipes courtesy of The Rare Fruit and Vegetable Council of Broward County, Florida

Recipe tester and food stylist: Stevie Bass, Food Concepts, Mill Valley, CA

Consultants

We thank the following people for contributing information or for checking the manuscript for accuracy:

Mary Lu Arpaia, Gary Bender, Robert Bergh, James Beutel, Rob Brokaw, John Brown, Tony Brown, Carl Campbell, Bob Chambers, C. Collins, Tom Cooper, R. E. Coronel, Norman Ellstrand, George Emerich, Jim Gilbert, Tom Gleason, Francis Gouin, Rudy Haluza, Tom Del Hotal, Gene Joyner, Ron Kadish, Robert Kurle, Richard Langdon, Kirk Larson, Brian Lievens, Paul Lyrene, Michael McConkey, Louis Migley, Dan Milbocker, John Moore, Jim Neitzel, Dorothy Nichols, Robert Norton, Jan Pirzio-Biroli, Gayther Plummer, John Riley, Chris Rollins, Kay Ryego, Dale Sato, C. C. Schaller, Art Schroeder, James B. Shanks, Wayne Sherman, Bob Smith, Steven Spangler, Jerry Staedeli, W. B. Storey, Jack Swords, J. L. Tayor, Paul Thompson, Ronald Tukey, Wm. F. Whitman, Horace Whittaker, Kathleen Williams, William Wiltbank.

Special Thanks To

John Arndt
Joan Byko, Contra Costa Solariums, Danville, CA
Deborah Cowder
Donald F. Dillon Sr., Four Winds Growers, Fremont, CA
George Emerich, Fallbrook, CA
Filoli Center, Woodside, CA
Milana Hames
Hearst Castle, San Simeon, CA
The Indoor Citrus and Rare Fruit Society
Michael Thomas Issel
Marilyn and Robert Singer
Angel Tardy
Paul Thomson, Bounsall, CA
University of California, Riverside

Photo Acknowledgments

(Names of photographers are followed by the page numbers on which their work appears. R = right, L = left, T = top, B = bottom)

William C. Aplin: 10L, 30, 34L, 61, 63, 74TR, 75TC
M. Badgley: 83L, 83TR, 83BR
Jen and Des Bartlett/Bruce Coleman, Inc.: 75L
Laurie Black: 14, 28, 29, 32L, 32R, 33L, 33TR, 38BL, 38BR, 39T, 39BL, 39BR, 41L, 41C, 42L, 43R, 54, 60, 88
Rick Bolen: 59T
California Avocado Commission/Produce Marketing Association: 18
Tom Cooper: 59B
Alan Copeland: 27, 76
Al Crozier: 34R
Dana Downie: 4, 21, 22L, 49BL, 92B
Lucy Erickson: 12B, 36C, 90
Ricardo Ferro/Black Star: 9
Charles M. Fitch/Shostal Associates: 69C
Four-By-Five: 7T
Douglas P. Garrabrants/Calavo: 17T, 17B
Bob Gossington/Bruce Coleman, Inc.: 69R
H. Armstrong Roberts: 51
Grant Heilman Photography: 8
Stefan Hames: 12T
Gene Joyner: 44B, 49R, 56L, 56R, 85R, 85BL
Michael Landis: 46T
Harvey Lloyd/Peter Arnold, Inc.: 7D
Michael McKinley: 89
M. Timothy O'Keefe/Bruce Coleman, Inc.: 10R
Ortho Photo Library: 6R, 7C, 40R, 65, 68, 73TL, 75B, Back cover TL, BL
Marcella Pedone/Shostal Associates: Back cover TR
J. Pehrson: 85TL
Pam Peirce: Front cover, 16, 23, 24L, 24TR, 24BR, 26TL, 26TR, 26BL, 26BR, 35TL, 35BL, 35R, 36TL, 36BL, 36TR, 36BR, 37L, 37R, 38T, 40L, 41R, 42C, 42R, 43L, 43C, 69L, Back cover BR
Chris Rollins: 1, 5, 6L, 46B, 66, 70, 71, 72, 73TR, 74TL, 74TC, 74B
B. Rothenberger: 84BR
Kjell B. Sandved/Bruce Coleman, Inc.: 73TC
Carlo Sanuvo/Bruce Coleman, Inc.: 75TR
Barry Shapiro: 52, 91, 92T
Ron Shunk: 22R, 55, 58, 64
Michael D. Smith: 84L
Joy Spur/Bruce Coleman, Inc.: 49TL
University of California: 84TR
Wardene Weisser/Bruce Coleman, Inc.: 44T, 57
Rod Whitlow: 31T

Chevron Chemical Company
575 Market Street, San Francisco, CA 94105

All About
C·I·T·R·U·S
& Subtropical Fruits

New and Familiar

Subtropical fruits may be as novel as the cherimoya, or as familiar as the navel orange. Whether they are borne on trees, shrubs, or vines, these fruits add richness to the landscape and excitement to the table.
Page 5

Understanding Your Climate

Subtropical fruits may be grown in almost any climate when given proper care. This chapter describes the climates where these fruits are found and shows how to modify a garden to provide the best growing conditions.
Page 9

The Best Subtropical Fruits

Subtropical fruits vary tremendously in flavor, landscape value, and growing requirements. Use this section to help you choose the best species and varieties for your garden and table.
Page 15

Caring for Subtropical Fruits

Subtropical fruits, like other plants, will thrive when given proper care. In this section, you'll find all you need to know about soils, fertilizers, watering, pruning, planting, propagation, and pest control.
Page 77

Subtropical Fruits in Containers

Container plantings offer the gardener versatility and opportunity. Many plants that would not survive if planted in the garden will thrive in containers.
Page 89

New and Familiar

Subtropical fruits may be as novel as the cherimoya, or as familiar as the navel orange. Whether they are borne on trees, shrubs, herbs, or vines, these fruits add richness to the landscape and excitement to the table.

Subtropical fruits generate a special kind of excitement for gardeners. Just let some of their names roll off your tongue: mango, papaya, banana, sapote, macadamia, passion fruit. These names call to mind faraway places and interesting new flavors. Even the familiar orange tree evokes images of sunny days, fragrant blossoms, and swaying palm trees. This romantic appeal is just one of the reasons that many gardeners are planting edible landscapes of subtropical plants.

Another reason for the increasing interest is that more subtropical fruits have begun to appear in supermarkets in recent years. And, as every gardener knows, if it tastes good from the supermarket, it will be even better if grown at home.

Although most subtropical fruits are usually imported, many others are now being grown in the United States. As more gardeners grow subtropical fruits, the foundation of experience grows, new techniques are developed, and everyone's chance of success improves. Today, home gardeners from California to Florida are growing subtropical fruits with increasing success.

Gardeners in cold climates are

Left: *Subtropical fruits in the landscape—exotic, elegant, and edible. The citrus trees in this garden are (left to right): 'Minneola' tangelo, 'Eureka' lemon, and 'Valencia' orange.*

Right: *Wonderful flavors can be contained in unfamiliar skins. These 'Gefner' atemoyas are described on page 25.*

not being left out. Many of these plants will bear fruit in greenhouses, or outdoors if protected in the winter.

What Are Subtropical Fruits?

This book introduces a world of new and unusual fruit. Some of the fruits included here are not truly subtropical. They may be tropical, native to areas close to the equator. Others could be considered temperate, native to areas with very cold winters. But all of them have one thing in common: They can be grown outdoors in the mild-winter areas of the United States, which can be broadly described as subtropical. These areas have some of the most desirable climates in the world, but gardeners living in many of them often cannot grow what we consider to be America's favorite fruits: apples, cherries,

peaches, and other plants that require cold winters for fruit production. For these gardeners, subtropical fruits are an unusual alternative.

Why Subtropical Fruits?

The most obvious reason for growing subtropical fruits is so you can enjoy fresh fruit, ripened to perfection. However, there are many other reasons for growing these plants.

Landscape Quality
The tropical landscape is one of the most appealing landscape designs. Large, bold leaves, fragrant flowers, and brightly colored fruit combine to create a tropical feeling sought by many gardeners and landscape architects. Many of the subtropical fruits described in this book are among the best plants for creating this tropical ambience. Few plants have the dramatic presence of the

banana, the year-round appeal of the strawberry guava, or the intense color of the passion flower. Some of these plants have a variety of uses in the landscape. Citrus can be pruned as a hedge or espaliered. Kiwi fruit and passion fruit vines can be trained to cover a fence or arbor. Figs make stunning shade trees. Also, many of these plants adapt well to containers.

The Challenge
Growing fruit of any kind takes a certain amount of commitment. Fruiting plants in general, whether they are apples, pears, or mangoes, are not usually considered low-maintenance plants. Also, the farther from ideal the growing condi-

tions are, the more attention the plants will need. But that challenge also makes success more rewarding. If you learn what a plant needs, provide the best possible planting site, and make special adjustments to allow it to thrive, your success will be all the more enjoyable.

On the other hand, some subtropical fruits are easy to grow in many areas. Citrus, figs, persimmons, and avocados are undemanding plants and, where adapted, provide abundant harvests with a minimum of attention.

Excitement at the Table
New flavors and fresh ingredients always make cooking and eating more exciting and enjoyable. For-

eign cuisines are more authentic, and often more delicious, when they are made with the same ingredients used by the people who developed them. Subtropical fruits are versatile and nutritious. Fresh lemons are a necessity for many cooks, and citrus is well known for its vitamin C content, but the more unusual subtropical fruits also have great nutritive and culinary value. Papayas contain an enzyme that is supposed to aid digestion, avocados

Left: *Four different* Eugenia *fruits (left to right):* Eugenia luschnathiana, Eugenia uniflora, Eugenia brasiliensis, Eugenia aggregata.

Below: *In addition to producing spectacular blossoms, many passion vines bear edible fruit. This vine,* Passiflora coccinea, *is described on page 67.*

Where Subtropical Fruits Are Native

1. AVOCADO—So. Mexico, Cent. America
2. BANANA—S.E. Asia
3. CHERIMOYA—Peru, Ecuador
4. FIG—Mediterranean region
5. FEIJOA—So. Brazil, Paraguay, Uruguay, No. Argentina
6. GUAVA—Columbia, Peru, Argentina
7. KIWI—China
8. LOQUAT—Cent. China, So. Japan
9. MACADAMIA—Australia
10. MANGO—India, S.E. Asia
11. LITCHI—So. China
12. PAPAYA—Cent. America
13. PASSION FRUIT—Brazil
14. JAPANESE PERSIMMON—Japan
15. TREE TOMATO—Peru
16. WHITE SAPOTE—Mexico, Cent. America
17. LIME—India, S.E. Asia
18. SOUR ORANGE—So. Vietnam
19. LEMON—S.E. Asia
20. PUMMELO—Malay Peninsula, Polynesia
21. CITRON—India
22. GRAPEFRUIT—West Indies
23. MANDARIN—S.E. Asia
24. SWEET ORANGE—China, So. Vietnam
25. WASHINGTON NAVEL—Brazil
26. KUMQUAT—So. China

contain vitamins A through K, and bananas are almost as rich in vitamins B and C as are oranges.

How to Use This Book

First, get to know how your climate affects the growth, adaptation, and productivity of subtropical fruits. The second chapter, "Understanding Your Climate," beginning on page 9, describes aspects of plant adaptation such as hardiness, heat requirements, and humidity requirements. It tells you how to take advantage of your garden's microclimates, so your plants will grow and yield bountiful harvests.

Next, get to know the most common subtropical fruits. In the third chapter, "The Best Subtropical Fruits," which begins on page 15, each fruit is described, with specific information on adaptation, propagation, site selection and planting, care requirements, harvest and storage, and suggestions for how the fruit can be used in the kitchen.

The basics of caring for subtropical fruit are found in the fourth chapter, "Caring for Subtropical Fruits," beginning on page 77. Here you'll find everything you need to know about soils, planting, watering, fertilizing, pest control, and propagation techniques.

The fifth chapter, "Subtropical Fruits in Containers," beginning on page 89, includes specific suggestions on how gardeners in cold-winter areas can successfully grow subtropical fruit indoors in the winter and outdoors in the summer, or in greenhouses.

The "Sources" section (page 94) is devoted to helping you find the varieties of subtropical fruit you want. It includes names and addresses of nurseries that specialize in subtropical fruits and organizations dedicated to their culture.

Top: *Citrus trees have long been prized for the beauty and fragrance of their blossoms.*

Center: *Pyramids of citrus fruits offer northern shoppers a year-round taste of warm, sunny climates.*

Bottom: *The trifoliate orange (Poncirus trifoliata) is a thorny plant with sour fruit, but it is a valuable rootstock used for dwarfing other species.*

Understanding Your Climate

Subtropical fruits may be grown in a variety of climates when given proper care. This chapter describes the climates suitable for subtropical fruits and shows how to modify a garden to provide the best microclimate.

The elements place severe restrictions on plants, and subtropical fruits are no exception. Your grapefruit will be sweet enough to eat only if the tree has absorbed enough sunlight and heat. Kiwi vines won't bloom satisfactorily if they don't get enough winter chilling. Cherimoyas will set more fruit if they flower in mild, humid weather, but mangoes must have warm, dry conditions while they are flowering to produce a crop.

Part of the gardener's art is to grow plants in areas where they wouldn't normally flourish. In order to meet this challenge, consider your climate and the needs of the plants you are growing.

Climate Variables

Each plant has a specific set of climatic requirements. These requirements are described in the "Adaptation" section of each plant description in this book. Some climatic requirements affect the survival of the plant; others affect fruit quality and productivity, but not necessarily survival.

Cold Tolerance

Each plant has a low-temperature limit, and will be damaged if exposed to temperatures below this limit. For many plants, this hardiness limit has been determined, and you can consult the USDA Plant Hardiness Zone Map on page 11 for a general impression of

Citrus are often planted on slopes rather than on the floor of a valley where cold air settles.

adaptation. Unfortunately, it's not easy to predict the performance of subtropical fruit species on the basis of the USDA Plant Hardiness Zone Map. Many subtropical plants carry their fruit through winter. Others bloom during cold months. Flowers and fruit are almost always less hardy than foliage and will usually be damaged if temperatures stay below freezing for very long.

On the brighter side, soil insulates roots against cold temperatures. So even if the top of a plant is killed, new shoots may sprout from the roots the following spring. Grafted trees will have to be regrafted, but seedling-grown plants will continue to produce the same fruit as before.

There are many ways you can protect plants from the cold, as shown in the illustrations on page 13. Plants that are *hardened off* (are growing at a reduced rate or are completely dormant due to exposure to cold) are hardier than those that are still growing actively. To encourage fall hardiness, avoid feeding tender plants with nitrogen fertilizers from mid- to late summer. Fertilization can encourage new growth that may be damaged by the first frost.

Heat Requirements

Next to damage from cold temperatures, insufficient warmth is the second greatest limiting factor to growing subtropical fruits. Without enough heat, bananas will just hang on the plant without ripening, and citrus won't sweeten. Passion fruit flowers will not set fruit. Papaya plants will rot at the base.

Each plant is affected differently, but the usual result of not having a long, warm summer is that the fruit will not ripen properly.

Some fruits are also damaged by too much heat. Several plants, including 'Washington' navel oranges and cherimoyas, will not set fruit in the heat of the desert Southwest. Many fruits are ruined by sunburn in very hot, arid climates.

Rainfall and Humidity

Atmospheric moisture affects plants in many ways. Abundant rainfall and high humidity ease your watering chores, but greatly increase the chances of fungal and bacterial diseases.

You can influence the humidity of your growing area by adjusting your watering schedule and method to weather conditions. To minimize disease problems in humid areas, avoid wetting the foliage and water in the morning so the soil surface will have a chance to dry before nightfall.

Some areas have borderline climates for citrus culture, but there are many ways to protect trees and prevent damage from frost. See page 13 for frost-protection methods.

Sunlight

Almost all the fruit species described in this book must be grown in full sun. Sunlight supplies the energy for manufacturing the plant sugars that will eventually make your fruit sweet and delicious. In desert areas, however, many plants benefit from partial shade during the hottest part of the day. Too much sunlight can also present a problem for recently pruned plants. To prevent sunburn, paint exposed branches and the trunk with water-based white paint (diluted 1 to 1) or commercially available tree paints.

Wind

Strong winds increase drought stress, break fruit-laden branches, and tear large leaves. The best way to protect wind-sensitive species is to plant them downwind of other, tougher species. Windbreaks are usually effective for a distance 10 times their height. Walls and solid fences aggravate wind problems, causing strong turbulence on both their windward and leeward sides.

Chilling Requirements

Several subtropical fruits, including kiwi fruit, figs, and persimmons, require exposure to a certain number of hours of temperatures between 32° and 45° F in winter. This is known as a plant's *chilling requirement*. Insufficient chilling causes plants to leaf out slowly and bloom irregularly. This can lead to sunburn and a general decline in vigor and yields. To expose a plant to maximum chilling, plant it in low spots or areas adjacent to a wall or fence at the bottom of a slope where cool air collects.

Varieties within a species often have different chilling requirements. "Low-chill" varieties are the only types of some fruit that can be grown in mild-winter climates.

Climate Regions

The climate of a region is influenced by a complex interaction of factors, including weather patterns, longitude, latitude, and topography. Also, a large body of water will moderate local climate. Generally, however, subtropical fruits can be grown in four main climate areas: tropical, semitropical, subtropical, and temperate.

Tropical Climates

Consistency is a major feature of tropical climates. Because there are no distinct seasons, one can expect abundant rainfall, high humidity, and warm temperatures throughout the year. Under such conditions, many plants act in a surprising way. Some grow actively 12 months of the year, often producing several crops. Oranges, for example, may flower four or five times in a year. You might think this would be a boon for tropical orange growers, but oranges do another odd thing in tropical areas—they stay green. Citrus develops its characteristic rind color only when the temperature drops below 45° F for an extended period, which it seldom does in tropical regions. This means an orange tree may be holding green fruit in four or five different stages of ripeness. Picking ripe fruit becomes a problem.

Many of the fruit described in this book are native to tropical areas of the world. Keeping in mind the consistent characteristics of tropical climates (such as Hawaii) should help you make these plants more at home in your garden.

Semitropical Climates

Southern Florida has a typical semitropical climate, and the areas along the Gulf Coast may also be included in this category. Humidity and annual rainfall are high, resembling tropical areas, but there are recognizable seasons. Summers are hot, and winters are generally warm with occasional cold spells. During some winters, cold Arctic air flows down from the north, often devastating tender plants.

Subtropical Climates

These areas are dramatically different from semitropical regions. The humidity may be very low in inland areas. Rainfall is often concentrated in the winter months and amounts to less than 10 inches a year in some areas.

Left: *The Cattley guava (*Psidium cattleianum*) is at its best in warm winter climates, but it will tolerate temperatures as low as 24° F.*

Below: *Smudge pots are often used for frost protection in commercial citrus orchards. The convective air movement produced by the pots keeps cold air from settling onto the trees.*

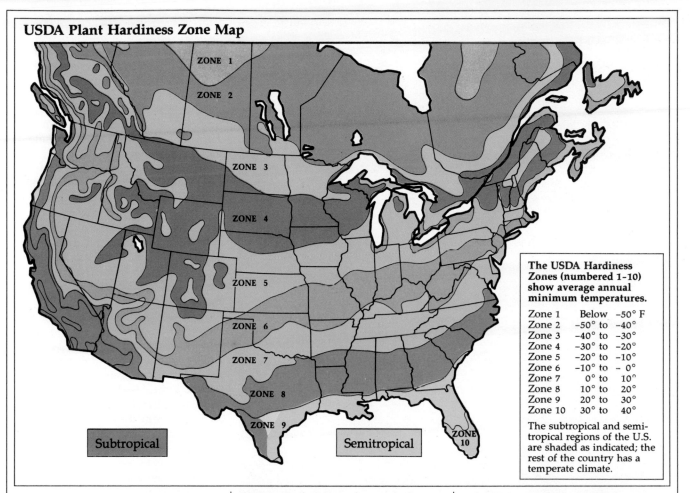

USDA Plant Hardiness Zone Map

ZONE 1
ZONE 2
ZONE 3
ZONE 4
ZONE 5
ZONE 6
ZONE 7
ZONE 8
ZONE 9
ZONE 10

Subtropical   Semitropical

The USDA Hardiness Zones (numbered 1-10) show average annual minimum temperatures.

Zone 1	Below	–50° F
Zone 2	–50° to	–40°
Zone 3	–40° to	–30°
Zone 4	–30° to	–20°
Zone 5	–20° to	–10°
Zone 6	–10° to	– 0°
Zone 7	0° to	10°
Zone 8	10° to	20°
Zone 9	20° to	30°
Zone 10	30° to	40°

The subtropical and semitropical regions of the U.S. are shaded as indicated; the rest of the country has a temperate climate.

Although subtropical climates are generally found in the low-elevation regions of California and Arizona, there is great variation among areas within these regions. Southern California and inland desert areas are hot and dry with relatively warm winters. Farther north, the winters are colder, rainier, and frosts are common. There are frost-free areas near the coast, but these are generally cool throughout the year because of their proximity to the Pacific Ocean. The inland valleys can be quite warm in summer.

Temperate Climates
Temperate climates are found throughout most of the United States. These climates generally have well-defined seasons, but the length of the seasons and their extremes differ according to latitude and local geographical features. To grow the plants in this book successfully in these climates, you will need to move them to a protected area in the winter. See the chapter, "Subtropical Fruits in Containers," beginning on page 89.

From Large to Small Climate Regions
The climates described in the previous paragraphs are the climates of your town, your county, or even your state. There is little you can do to change them. There are, however, things you can do to alter *microclimates*, the distinct climates around your home that are slightly different from the general climate of your area.

Solar energy, the prime mover of all weather, is an impressive force. You can take advantage of the different ways this energy is absorbed and reflected to modify the microclimate of your garden to suit the needs of your plants.

Radiation Principles
The heat of sunlight may be either desirable or undesirable, depending on where you live, the season, and the plants you would like to grow.

As light and heat come from the sun to your garden, a variety of things happen. Part of the energy is reflected into space from clouds over the earth, part of it is scattered and diffused as it strikes small par-

ticles in the earth's atmosphere, and part of it is absorbed by carbon dioxide, water vapor, and ozone in the atmosphere. The remainder, approximately one fifth, penetrates directly through the atmosphere to the earth's surface, where it is either absorbed or reflected.

As a result, the plants in your yard may receive solar energy as reflected radiation from atmospheric particles, as reflected radiation from materials on or near the earth's surface, or as direct radiation from the sun.

Absorption, Radiation, and Reflection   At night the earth radiates some of the heat it absorbed during the day. Materials vary in the amount of radiation they store, depending on their composition. Loose, organic mulches, for example, store much less heat than gravel mulches.

Because light surfaces reflect more than dark ones, the color of a material is a microclimatic control. Dark surfaces absorb more heat that can be released later. Light-colored objects reflect more heat and light. By planting next to a

Top: *A few 150-watt light bulbs at the base of a covered plant can add enough heat to protect it from a potentially damaging frost.*

Bottom: *Light-colored paving at the base of these 'Eureka' lemon trees reflects light and heat into the foliage and fruit.*

light-colored wall, you can maximize the amount of heat a plant receives during the day. Conversely, a plant next to a dark-colored wall stays warmer at night.

Exposure   At most latitudes in the northern hemisphere, the south side of a home will receive the most sun the year around. The east side will bask in morning light, the west side will receive the hottest afternoon sun, and the north side will be shaded much of the time. Of course, the light intensity changes with the seasons, but in general, if you want maximum heat, plant on the southern or western side of your home.

Frost Protection

Any tender plant can be successfully protected against cold if you are willing to try hard enough. Many gardeners plant in containers and move their fruit trees indoors during the winter (see page 93). Others construct plastic covers to trap heat radiating from the soil or bury their plants in protective mulches. But in many areas the most important thing is to recognize cold spots in the garden and select the warmest possible planting site.

Plants can be damaged by two types of cold weather: *radiation frosts* and *advective freezes*. Radiation frosts occur on cool, clear, still nights when plants and the objects around them radiate heat to the sky. Water may condense on the leaves if the humidity is high enough, but the plants can be damaged even if no visible frost condenses. To avoid radiation frost damage, plant sensitive species next to a south-facing wall that will store heat during the day and release it at night. A roof overhang above the plants will reduce the amount of heat radiated to the sky and provide additional protection. Canvas and plastic covers will also protect plants from radiation frost damage. The heat radiated from the soil will help keep the plant warm. Also, avoid planting in low spots, where cold air settles.

Advective freezes occur over a wide area as a result of an influx of Arctic air. Such freezes are common in Florida and Texas. The techniques used to protect against radiation frosts will also protect plants in advective freezes.

Frost-Protection Methods

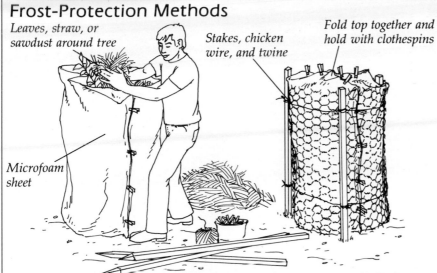

Leaves, straw, or sawdust around tree

Microfoam sheet

Stakes, chicken wire, and twine

Fold top together and hold with clothespins

Enclose a small tree in a cylinder of waterproof microfoam filled with a dry insulating material, such as leaves, straw, or sawdust. Support the cylinder with stakes and chicken wire.

A frame covered with plastic will protect a tree. The foliage should not touch the plastic. Light bulbs provide additional heat.

Pull mulch back to expose soil to sunlight. The heat radiated from the soil at night will provide some protection.

Gravel stores even more heat than open soil. Add a stone mulch to create a more efficient heat sink.

Protect the trunk by mounding mulch around it. If the top is damaged, the trunk will resprout.

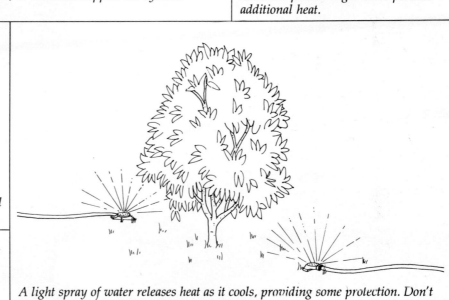

A light spray of water releases heat as it cools, providing some protection. Don't let the spray hit the foliage—the water will freeze on the branches and the weight may break them. Make sure the water can drain away.

Move sensitive container-grown plants indoors or to a protected location.

New, polymer-based antitranspirant sprays may give several degrees of frost protection.

The Best Subtropical Fruits

Subtropical fruits vary widely in flavor, landscape value, and growing requirements. Use this section to help you choose the best species and varieties for your garden and table.

The following encyclopedia describes more than 40 subtropical fruits. The 17 most important fruits are described in detail; the others are in the charts on pages 73-75.

Each of the 17 major fruit descriptions contains a quick reference chart. At the top of this chart is a map showing the areas where the plant is well adapted (red) and marginally adapted (yellow). In marginal areas, choose hardy varieties if available and plant in protected areas. It's important to remember that these maps are for quick reference only. More precise information is included in the "Adaptation" section of each description and in the chapter entitled "Understanding Your Climate," beginning on page 9.

The information in the chart below the adaptation map includes descriptions of the plant's growth habit, harvest season, ornamental quality, and suitability for container culture. The last two entries in the chart, "Nurseries" and "Information," are probably the most important. They are keyed to lists of nurseries and organizations on page 94. These nurseries and organizations can supply you with both additional information and plants. All of the plant species described in this book are available from one or more of the nursery sources, but some varieties of each species are harder to find than others; you may need to contact several nurseries to find the one you want.

Subtropical fruits grace your table as well as your garden.

These descriptions include information on adaptation, pollination, propagation, site selection, watering, fertilizing, pruning, pest and disease control, harvesting and storing, and tips on how to enjoy the fruit at the table.

Harvest Periods
The harvest periods listed in the fruit descriptions are only general guidelines. To adapt these guidelines to your area, remember that fruit will ripen earlier in warmer areas than in cooler locations.

New Flavors
Some of the fruit described in the following sections are undeniably delicious. Mangoes, papayas, blood oranges, cherimoyas, and many others, although they may be new to you, will be an absolute pleasure to eat. In many cases we have included recipes for you to try.

Some of the subtropical fruits, such as tree tomatoes and passion fruit, may seem a bit strange at first. You may find them more palatable in preserves or cooked in recipes. The important thing is to give yourself time to enjoy these fruits and to experiment with new ways to use them.

Selected Varieties
Most plants grown from seed are genetically unique, different in major or minor ways from all other plants of the same species. They may have better fruit quality, a different plant habit, a wider range of adaptation, or a darker leaf. These differences are the basis of natural selection and the survival

of the fittest. In their native habitats, plants that possess certain advantages are better competitors and are more likely to survive.

On a horticultural level, plants that have desirable characteristics are vegetatively propagated and called *selected varieties* or *cultivars*. Selected varieties of each subtropical fruit, if any, are shown in the charts with each plant description. Unless a plant breeds true from seed, selected varieties should always be your first choice. When you purchase a selected variety, you are assured it will have the superior fruit quality or the specific adaptation of its parent.

Pollination
The pollination requirements of subtropical fruits deserve special attention. Species and varieties that set fruit without another tree nearby are called *self-fruitful*. These plants either provide their own pollen or else their flowers do not require pollination to set fruit. Species or varieties that must be pollinated by another, different variety are called *self-unfruitful*. In the absence of natural pollinators (such as bees or flies), some fruit must be hand-pollinated. This is usually the case with cherimoyas and can be a problem with many plants grown in greenhouses. The specific pollination requirements of each fruit are included in the encyclopedia.

If space is limited, consider grafting a pollinator limb onto a tree rather than planting two trees. For more about grafting, see the section entitled "Propagating Subtropical Fruits," which begins on page 85.

Avocado

Avocados are generally large, dominating trees that, under the proper conditions, provide an abundant harvest of rich, buttery fruit.

Three races of avocado are in cultivation: Mexican, Guatemalan, and West Indian, as well as hybrids of these groups. The Mexican, Guatemalan, and hybrids of the two are best adapted to California and cold areas of the Southeast. West Indian varieties are best adapted to southern Florida and Hawaii. Although there are great similarities between groups, Mexican varieties are generally hardier and bear fruit with a smoother and thinner shiny green or black skin. Guatemalan avocados are restricted almost exclusively to frost-free climates and bear blackish-green fruit with a thick, bumpy rind. West Indian varieties are the most frost sensitive and have thin, smooth, greenish-yellow skin.

Avocado fruits vary from round to pear shaped, depending on the variety. They may be as small as 4 ounces or as large as 2 pounds. Because these varieties ripen at different times of the year, there are almost always avocados in the supermarket.

Avocado trees can become quite large under ideal growing conditions and may live 20 or more years. They are stately trees when used as a single specimen, but are generally too large for small gardens. Mature foliage is deep green and leathery. New growth is coppery red, appearing in flushes throughout the year. The leaves of Mexican varieties have a scent like anise. The flowers are yellowish white and are borne in clusters.

Avocado varieties differ in flavor. A high oil content usually means rich flavor.

Adaptation

Avocados are widely grown in the mild-winter areas of Florida, California, and Hawaii. Some hardier varieties can also be grown in cooler parts of northern and inland California and along the Gulf Coast. See page 19 for a chart showing the common varieties and their areas of adaptation.

Although the foliage of the hardiest Mexican varieties can withstand temperatures as low as 24° F, the fruit and flowers are less hardy and will be damaged at higher temperatures. Cool weather during bloom can limit fruit set. High temperatures after fruit set may cause excessive fruit drop.

Lack of adequate soil drainage is often the most important limiting factor in growing avocados. Poorly drained soils or the constantly wet soils common in the Southeast can kill a tree.

Pollination

Most avocados are self-fruitful. In California, however, by combining the right varieties you can increase yields. Avocado flowers are classed as type A or type B. Varieties with type A flowers are receptive to pollen in the morning, but don't release their pollen until the afternoon of the following day. The situation is reversed with Type B avocados: The flowers are receptive in the afternoon but the pollen isn't released until the following morn-

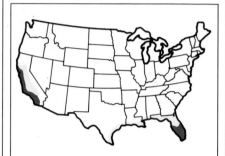

Common Name: Avocado, alligator pear, love fruit.

Botanical Name: *Persea americana.*

Origin: Tropical regions of Central America.

Growth Habit: Evergreen tree. 20 to 60 feet high, 25 to 35 feet wide. Moderate growth rate.

Adaptation: Hardiness varies according to variety; ranges from 18 to 30 feet. Specific varieties are recommended for Florida, California, or Hawaii.

Harvest Season: Fruit matures on different varieties throughout the year. Available in supermarkets throughout the year.

Begins Bearing: Grafted plants bear in 2 to 3 years. Seedlings bear fruit of variable quality in 8 to 12 years.

Propagation: Named varieties are grafted to clonal or seedling rootstocks.

Maintenance: Low.

Pollination: Self-fruitful. Cross-pollination of varieties with A and B flower types may improve yields in California (see "Pollination," above).

Suitability for Containers: Select semidwarf varieties. Requires at least a 15-gallon container.

Landscape Quality: Good but casts deep shade. Mature trees too large for small gardens.

Nurseries: I, M, O, P, Q, U, Y.

Information: 1, 2, 4, 8, 13, 14.

Below: *These 'Hass' avocados will be ready to pick when they just begin to turn black.*

ing. Combining varieties with different flower types ensures that plenty of pollen is available when flowers are most receptive, and results in high yields, although a single tree will produce enough fruit for most families.

If space is limited, either graft pollenizer limbs onto the desired variety or plant more than one tree in a single hole. Semidwarf varieties are also useful in small gardens.

Propagation

The seed in any avocado will usually germinate. It can take years, however, before a seedling will bear fruit, and the quality will probably be inferior to the fruit of the parent tree. Seedlings can be used as rootstocks for grafting your own tree unless you live in an area where avocado root rot is a problem. In such areas it is best to plant varieties grafted to root rot–resistant rootstocks, such as 'Duke 7', but even these won't ensure success.

Seedlings are ready to graft when they reach ¼ to ⅜ inch in diameter. Obtain budwood from dormant terminal growth, which is just starting to swell in the spring. Remove the leaves to keep the wood from drying out.

Cleft or veneer grafting or chip and shield budding are common methods for propagating avocados. See pages 86-87 for the techniques.

Older, established trees can be topworked, a method where shoots of a new variety are grafted onto the main branches of a mature tree.

Site Selection and Planting

Plant avocados in deep, well-drained soil in an area with full sun. The trees will not tolerate standing water and have a low tolerance for soil salts. A pH of 5.5 to 6.5 is ideal. Choose a site where the tree will have room to spread.

Spring is the best time to plant. Plant the tree so its crown is slightly higher than it was in the nursery container, to allow for settling.

Top: 'Hass', a popular rough-skinned avocado variety.

Bottom: 'Fuerte', a smooth-skinned avocado variety.

Caring for Avocado Trees

Watering   The most important aspect of growing avocados successfully is careful watering. As is usually the case with plants that are very sensitive to soil moisture levels, too much water is as dangerous as not enough. A soil auger or sampling tube will go a long way in helping you determine when to water. Feeder roots, the ones most sensitive to overly wet soil, are concentrated in the top 15 inches of soil. Allow this zone to dry partially before watering mature trees. Avocado trees will survive with less water, but for a quality harvest in dry climates, you will probably have to water deeply every 2 to 4 weeks. Young trees will, of course, need more frequent watering, probably every week or two depending on the weather.

Use a basin to direct water to the root zone, making sure to increase the size of the basin as the tree grows. Break the walls of the basin to provide drainage during rainy seasons. An organic mulch, 3 to 6 inches deep and kept 12 inches away from the trunk, will help keep feeder roots cool.

Fertilizing   From early spring to late summer, apply small amounts of a complete fertilizer. Young trees that are growing slowly can be fed with a complete fertilizer according to the label instructions. In cold climates do not fertilize after late summer to allow the trees to become cold-hardy.

Avocados often show signs of iron deficiency (yellowing of the new growth), especially in soils with a high pH. Correct with soil applications of iron chelate and add sulfur to lower the soil pH.

Pruning   Avocados require little pruning other than shaping when young and removal of dead or misplaced branches as they mature.

Trees can, however, be pruned regularly to keep them within bounds. In fact, a fully mature avocado tree can be cut back to a 3-foot stump (make sure to cut above the graft union); it will usually bear fruit again in 3 years. If you try this, select the strongest of the new shoots and remove any weak growth or misplaced branches. The new shoots may need staking to prevent them from breaking in strong winds.

Pests and Diseases   Avocado root rot is a major disease problem in California. Select disease-free, certified plants and avoid planting where avocados once grew or where soil drainage is poor. The disease is easily transported by equipment, tools, and shoes from infected soils to uninfected soils. Once a tree is infected (signs include yellowing and dropping leaves), there is little you can do but cut back on water. Snails can be a problem in California.

In the humid Southeast, fungus diseases such as scab, anthracnose, and powdery mildew are common. Scale, looper worms, mites, borers, and thrips may attack avocados, but they are usually not serious enough to require chemical control.

Harvest and Storage

Knowing exactly when to pick an avocado can be tricky. The length of time from pollination to harvest differs according to variety. A 'Fuerte' avocado usually requires 8 to 10 months, but a 'Hass' avocado needs 13 to 14 months. The fruit of some varieties can be stored on the tree to supply high-quality, flavorful fruit for 9 to 20 weeks. Other varieties have a very short period (from 6 to 8 weeks) of peak flavor. Overly mature fruit will soften on the tree and develop an "off" flavor. In hot summer months, the fruit matures more quickly than in cooler winter months. In any case the fruit must be picked when mature but still hard, and ripened off the tree. Immature fruit will wrinkle, won't soften evenly, and will have poor flavor.

Dark varieties will begin to turn from green to black when they are ready to be picked. Green varieties will develop a yellowish tinge. When you think the fruit are beginning to ripen, pick one of the larger ones and allow it to ripen in a paper bag with a banana or an apple. When ripe, the fruit will feel soft under gentle pressure. Remove the flesh and check the seed coat, a thin membrane that covers the seed. A dark brown, paper-thin seed coat is a good sign of a mature fruit. Immature fruit will have a light tan or yellow seed coat.

Use hand-held pruning shears to harvest the fruit, leaving a small piece of stem attached. This helps prevent decay during ripening or storage. For tall trees, you'll probably need a ladder or collapsible-extension fruit harvester, available in many nurseries.

Avocados at the Table

If you are an avocado fancier, you know how wonderful a ripe avocado is simply halved, sprinkled with salt, pepper, and lime juice, and eaten with a spoon. For a more elegant presentation, fan slices on a bed of greens with various fruits, garnish with capers, and dress with vinaigrette. Remember that once

Smooth and spicy guacamole is the perfect answer to a bumper crop of avocados.

cut, avocado browns rapidly and should be coated with lemon or lime juice to prevent discoloration.

Guacamole is probably the most popular avocado dish. There are many versions of guacamole, but most are made of avocados mashed with bits of ripe tomato, lime juice, salt, hot red pepper flakes, cumin, chopped cilantro, and minced onion. Serve guacamole with tortilla chips or raw vegetables, or use it to garnish bowls of chili, enchiladas, or turkey sandwiches. For a rich and impressive first course or luncheon entrée, try the following recipe for Avocado Soup.

Avocado Soup

- 4 cups chicken stock, preferably homemade
- ¼ cup butter
- 1 clove garlic, minced
  Half a medium yellow onion, diced (½ cup)
- ¼ cup unbleached all-purpose flour
- 1 teaspoon cumin, ground
- 1 teaspoon grated orange rind
- ¼ teaspoon cayenne pepper
- 2 ripe avocados (1 pound)
- 1 cup sour cream
  Cilantro and/or diced cucumber, for garnish

1. Bring chicken stock to a simmer.

2. Meanwhile, in a 2-quart (or larger) saucepan, melt butter and sauté garlic and onion until onion is translucent. Add flour and cook over medium heat, stirring continuously with a wire whisk, until the flour just begins to turn golden.

3. Slowly pour in hot chicken stock and cook, stirring, until soup begins to thicken. Blend in cumin, orange rind, and cayenne.

4. Peel, seed, and dice the avocados. Combine with soup and ½ cup of the sour cream in an electric blender or food processor and process until smooth. (Process in batches, if necessary.) Add salt to taste.

5. Soup may be served either warm or chilled. To serve warm, return soup to saucepan and heat.

6. Serve garnished with remaining ½ cup sour cream, some cilantro, and, if soup is chilled, cucumber. For best color, serve the same day.

Serves 6.

Avocado Varieties

VARIETY*	FRUIT DESCRIPTION	COMMENTS
Varieties for California		
Anaheim (A)	Large to very large, green, fair flavor. Ripens June to August.	Fairly small, upright tree. Hardy to 32° F.
Fuerte (B)	Small to medium, green, excellent flavor. Ripens November to June.	Large, spreading tree. Hardy to 28° F. Production somewhat erratic.
Hass (A)	Small to medium, purple to black, with excellent, nutty flavor.	Ripens February to October. Medium-large tree. Hardy to 30° F. Alternate bearing.
Jim (B)	Small to medium, green, very good flavor. Ripens September to January.	Medium, upright tree. Hardy to 24° F. Heavy producer.
Mexicola (A)	Small, purple, with very good, nutty flavor. Ripens August to October.	Medium, spreading tree. Hardy to 18° F. Heavy producer.
Nabal (B)	Medium, green, excellent flavor. Ripens June to October.	Large, upright tree. Hardy to 30° F. Erratic but heavy producer.
Pinkerton (A)	Small to medium, green, very good flavor. Ripens October to January.	Medium, slightly spreading tree. Hardy to 30° F. Heavy producer.
Reed (A)	Medium to large, green, excellent flavor. Ripens June to November.	Medium, upright tree. Hardy to 30° F. Heavy producer.
Zutano (B)	Medium, green, good flavor. Ripens December to January.	Large, very upright tree. Hardy to 26° F. Heavy producer.
Varieties for Florida		
Booth 7	Medium to large, green, good flavor. Ripens October to December.	Medium, spreading tree.
Brogdin	Small to medium, dark purple, very good flavor. Ripens July to September.	Medium, upright tree. Hardy to 22° F.
Choquette	Large to very large, green, very good flavor. Ripens November to February.	Medium, spreading tree resists scab disease. Hardy to 26° F.
Gainesville	Small, green. Ripens July to August.	Medium, upright tree. Hardy to 18° F.
Hall	Large to very large, green, good flavor. Ripens November to January.	Medium tree. Hardy to 28° F. Heavy producer.
Lula	Medium to large, green, good flavor. Ripens November to February.	Large, upright tree. Hardy to 25° F. Primarily a commercial variety.
Mexicola	Small, black, fair flavor. Ripens July to August.	Medium tree. Hardy to 18° F. Good for northern areas.
Monroe	Large, green, good flavor. Ripens November to January.	Medium tree. Hardy to 26° F.
Pollock	Large to very large, green, very good flavor. Ripens July to September.	Medium, spreading tree resists scab disease. Hardy to 32° F. Light producer.
Simmonds	Large to very large, green, very good flavor. Ripens July to September.	Medium, spreading tree resists scab disease. Hardy to 32° F. Heavy producer.
Tonnage	Medium to large, green fruit, good flavor. Ripens September to October.	Tall, upright tree. Hardy to 25° F. Good for colder areas.
Waldin	Medium, green, very good flavor. Ripens September to October.	Large, upright tree resists scab disease. Hardy to 32° F.
Varieties for Hawaii		
Beardslee	Large, green, good flavor. Ripens in winter.	Extremely large, productive, upright tree.
Case	Medium to very large, green, very good flavor. Ripens in winter.	Medium tree. Good producer.
Chang	Medium to large, green, very good flavor. Ripens in spring.	Medium tree. Consistently heavy producer.
Frowe	Medium to large, purple, very good flavor. Ripens in late fall.	Medium tree. Good producer.
Greengold	Medium to large, green, excellent flavor. Ripens winter to spring.	Medium, spreading tree. Heavy producer.
Hayes	Medium to large, purple, very good flavor. Ripens winter to spring.	Medium tree. Good producer. Susceptible to mites.
Kahaluu	Medium to large, green, excellent flavor. Ripens late fall to winter.	Medium to large, upright tree. Light producer. Susceptible to thrips and mites.
Masami	Medium, purple, very good flavor. Ripens winter to spring.	Medium, upright tree. Good producer.
Murashige	Medium to very large, green, excellent flavor. Ripens spring to summer.	Medium, upright tree. Tends to bear heavily in alternate years. Handsome habit.
Nishikawa	Medium to very large, green, very good flavor. Ripens early winter to spring.	Medium tree. Good producer.
Ohata	Large to very large, purple, very good flavor. Ripens spring to summer.	Medium tree. Light producer.
Sharwil	Small to medium, green, excellent flavor. Ripens winter to spring.	Medium, spreading tree. Bears heavily in alternate years.
Dwarf Varieties for Containers and Small Gardens* *		
Gwen (A)	Small, green, excellent flavor. Ripens March to November.	Small, compact, upright tree to 12 to 14 feet high. Hardy to 30° F. Heavy producer.
Little Cado*** (Wurtz)	Small, green, good flavor. Ripens May to September.	Very small, compact tree reaches 8 to 10 feet high. Hardy to 32° F. Light producer.
Whitsell (B)	Small, green, excellent flavor. Ripens March to July.	Small, compact tree to 12 feet. Hardy to 30° F. Bears heavily in alternate years.

*Letter in parentheses indicates flower type (see page 16). **Available in California. ***Type unknown.*

Banana

Bananas and their relatives are staple food for most tropical countries. There are many species of banana, but the edible types were developed by crossing and recrossing two species: *Musa acuminata* and *Musa balbisiana*. *Musa acuminata* is a sweet banana; *Musa balbisiana* is starchier but is more vigorous and resistant to disease. Most of the commonly available varieties are seedless hybrids of the two species and usually resemble one parent more than the other. For instance, the finest bananas for fresh eating, such as 'Cavendish', resemble *Musa acuminata*. Cooking bananas, commonly called plantains, are closer to *Musa balbisiana*.

Banana plants are extremely decorative, ranking next to palm trees

Common Name: Banana.

Botanical Name: Hybrids of *Musa acuminata* and *Musa balbisiana*.

Origin: Southeast Asia.

Growth Habit: Fast-growing, upright, herbaceous perennial 5 to 25 feet high. Huge, tropical-looking leaves. Spreads by underground rhizomes.

Adaptation: Freezing temperatures will kill the foliage. Rhizomes are hardy to 22° F. Requires ample fertilizer, water, and heat. Dwarf varieties are also available.

Harvest Season: Within 4 to 8 months after flowering.

Begins Bearing: Within 12 to 18 months after planting.

Propagation: By division of rhizomes or from suckers.

Maintenance: Moderate.

Pollination: Self-fruitful.

Suitability for Containers: Well suited. Excellent indoors in bright, diffused light.

Landscape Quality: Excellent. Beautiful tropical appearance. Frequently used as landscape plants.

Nurseries: E, I, O, P, Q, U, W, X.

Information: 1, 2, 3, 14.

for the wonderful tropical feeling they lend to the landscape. Technically, they are herbaceous perennials arising from underground rhizomes. The fleshy stalks sheathed with huge, broad leaves can rise 5 to 25 feet in as little as six months, depending on the variety. Each stalk produces one huge flower cluster, which develops fruit, then dies. New stalks then grow from the rhizome. Fruit size and flavor vary considerably, but most home garden varieties are 4 to 8 inches long and very sweet. The clusters of fruit may weigh more than 100 pounds.

Adaptation

Bananas grow best in a uniformly warm climate, and require 10 to 15 months of frost-free conditions to produce a flower stalk. The fruit takes 4 to 8 months to mature, depending on the temperature. All

Few plants say "tropical" as strongly as the banana.

but the hardiest varieties stop growing when the temperature drops below 53° F.

Freezing temperatures will kill a banana to the ground. If the temperature does not fall below 22° F, however, and the cold period is short, the underground rhizome will usually survive.

At the other end of the temperature scale, the ideal temperature for ripening fruit is around 80° F. The plants grow slowly above that point and stop growing entirely when the temperature reaches 100° F. High temperatures and bright sunlight will scorch leaves and fruit.

In most areas, bananas require wind protection for best appearance and maximum yield. The

Banana Varieties

VARIETY	HEIGHT	COMMENTS
Apple (Manzano, Go Sai Heong)	10 to 15 feet	Fingers 4 to 5 inches long with thin, yellow skin. 6 to 7 hands per 25- to 45-pound bunch. Flesh dry but has good flavor and an apple aroma. Astringent if not fully ripe.
Bluefields (Gros Michel, Pouyat, Martinique)	15 to 25 feet	Fingers 7 to 9 inches long with thick, bright yellow skin. 8 to 12 hands per 60- to 100-pound bunch. Excellent flavor. Very susceptible to Panama wilt.
Brazilian (Brazilian Apple, Park-Yuk, Pome)	15 to 25 feet	Fingers 4 to 6 inches long with yellow skin and distinct square beak. Yellow flesh with low-acid flavor.
Chinese (Dwarf Cavendish, Dwarf Chinese)	7 to 10 feet	Fingers 6 to 8 inches long with creamy yellow skin. 6 to 9 hands per 40- to 90-pound bunch. Sweet flavor. Good for Florida. Does not store well.
Cocos (Dwarf Bluefields)	10 to 15 feet	Fingers 5 to 7 inches long with bright yellow skin. 8 to 12 hands per 60- to 100-pound bunch. Excellent flavor, similar to that of 'Bluefields'.
Dwarf Brazilian (Santa Carina Prata)	10 to 15 feet	Fingers 5 to 6 inches long with yellow skin. 5 to 7 hands per 25- to 50-pound bunch. Flavor identical to that of 'Brazilian'.
Golden Aromatic	10 to 12 feet	Fingers 6 to 9 inches long with golden yellow skin. 4 to 5 hands per 30- to 40-pound bunch. Very good flavor, resembling that of 'Bluefields'. Stores well.
Golden Beauty (I.C. 2)	15 to 25 feet	Fingers 4 to 6 inches long with golden skin. 5 to 8 hands per 25- to 40-pound bunch. Keeps well.
Green Red	20 to 25 feet	Fingers 5 to 7 inches long with thick, dark purplish skin that turns yellow and red when ripe. 4 to 7 hands per 30- to 50-pound bunch. Good flavor. Trunks and fruit stems have light and dark green stripes.
Hamakau (Bungulan, Monte Cristo, Pisang Masak Hijau)	15 to 25 feet	Fingers 6 to 9 inches long with creamy yellow skin. 6 to 9 hands per 50- to 100-pound bunch. Flavor similar to that of 'Chinese'. Poor keeping quality.
Ice Cream (Java Blue)	10 to 15 feet	Fingers 5 to 6 inches long with bluish silver skin that turns pale yellow when ripe. 7 to 9 hands per 40- to 60-pound bunch. Sweet flavor. Good fresh or cooked.
Lady Finger (Ney Poovan)	20 to 25 feet	Fingers 4 to 5 inches long with thin, pale yellow skin. 10 to 14 hands per 40- to 65-pound bunch. Sweet white flesh. Flavor similar to that of 'Apple' and 'Mysore'.
Largo (Bluggoe)	8 to 10 feet	Fingers 7 to 9 inches long with thick, light yellow skin. 4 to 7 hands per 50- to 60-pound bunch. Pink flesh. Mild flavor when raw; usually cooked. Similar to 'Orinoco'.
Orinoco (Horse Burro, Better Select)	12 to 15 feet	Fingers 8 to 12 inches long. 5 to 9 hands per 40- to 50-pound bunches. Best flavor when fully ripe. Dry texture, usually cooked. Commonly grown in Florida. Good cold tolerance.
Philippines Lacatan	15 to 20 feet	Fingers 5 to 7 inches long. 6 to 8 hands per 40- to 60-pound bunch. Excellent flavor.
Plantain (Horse Plantain)	12 to 14 feet	Fingers 8 to 12 inches long. 5 to 9 hands per 40- to 60-pound bunch. Used for cooking.
Poovan (Father Lenore, Mysore)	25 feet	Fingers 4 to 6 inches long with light yellow skin. 8 to 10 hands per 50- to 60-pound bunch. Moist, pale yellow flesh. Very productive, cold tolerant. Low-acid flavor.
Red Cuban (Cuban Red, Red, Spanish Red, Colorado)	20 to 25 feet	Fingers 5 to 6 inches long with a thick, dark purple skin that turns red when ripe. Cream-colored flesh. Good flavor. Red foliage.
Sucrier (Ninio, Honey)	15 to 20 feet	Fingers 4 to 6 inches long with golden yellow skin. 6 to 7 hands per 25- to 45-pound bunch. Very sweet.
Valery (Taiwan, Tall Mons Mari)	10 to 15 feet	Fingers 7 to 10 inches long with yellow skin. 8 to 10 hands per 60- to 90-pound bunch. Good flavor. Cold tolerant.
Walha	10 to 15 feet	Fingers 5 to 7 inches long. 5 to 6 hands per 20- to 50-pound bunch. Low-acid flavor similar to that of 'Brazilian'. Erroneously called 'Dwarf Apple'.
Williams (Giant Cavendish, Giant Chinese, Mons Mari)	9 to 12 feet	Fingers 7 to 9 inches long with yellow skin and tapered tip. 9 to 12 hands per 60- to 90-pound bunch. Good flavor. Flowers won't develop in cool weather.

heavy fruit clusters, large leaves, and shallow roots combine to make bananas very susceptible to being blown over. Wind also tears the leaves.

Pollination
Bananas develop without pollination. The plant produces a long flower stalk with rows of female flowers called "hands." The fruit, or "fingers," first begin to develop at the base of the stalk (closest to where it originates from the plant). At first, the embryonic fruit point downward under a protective sheath. Then, when the sheath falls off and the fruit begin to develop, they curve upward.

The male flowers don't appear until all of the fruit have begun to grow. Although pretty, they take energy from the plant that would otherwise go into the developing fruit. For this reason, commercial banana growers cut the flower stalk off just below the last hand.

Site Selection and Planting
Bananas are usually sold as semi-dormant rhizomes or as container-grown suckers. If you purchase rhizomes, plant them close to the surface of a deep, well-drained soil rich in organic matter. The soil pH should be between 5.5 and 6.5. The banana is not tolerant of salty soils. The plants grow best in full sun.

Banana Varieties
The banana variety chart (left) lists the most common banana varieties, but other varieties have been bred for specific climates. Also, many varieties are known by different names, depending on where they are grown. The most common of these synonyms are listed after each preferred variety name.

Caring for Banana Plants
Watering   The huge leaves of a banana plant use a great deal of water. Regular, deep watering is absolutely necessary during warm weather. Do not let plants dry out, but don't overwater—standing water, especially in cool weather, will cause root rot. Spread a thick layer of mulch on the soil to conserve moisture, retard weeds, and protect the shallow roots.

In dry-summer climates, such as in Southern California, extra water should be used occasionally to leach out the accumulated soil salts.

Fertilizing   Their rapid growth rate makes bananas heavy feeders. During warm weather, apply a balanced fertilizer once a month. A mature plant may require as much as 1½ to 2 pounds of a 6 percent nitrogen fertilizer each month. Young plants need a quarter to a third as much.

Spread the fertilizer evenly around the plant in a circle extending 4 to 8 feet from the trunk. Do not allow the fertilizer to come in contact with the trunk.

Pruning   Only one primary stem on each rhizome should be allowed to fruit. All excess shoots should be removed as soon as they are noticed. This helps channel all of the plant's energy into fruit production. Once the main stalk is six to eight months old, permit one sucker to develop as a replacement stalk for the following season.

When the fruit is harvested, cut the fruiting stalk back to 30 inches above the ground. Remove the stub several weeks later. Dispose of the cut stems to prevent disease.

Pests and Diseases   Bananas have few troublesome pests or diseases outside tropical countries. The best way to avoid problems is to purchase disease-free plants from a reputable source and plant them in a well-drained soil.

Harvest and Storage

Bananas carried on the plant through the winter will mature quickly when warmer weather arrives. If you live in a cool area, you may want to cover fruit clusters with plastic or brown paper to increase the temperature of the fruit and hasten maturity. This can also help prevent sunburn and other blemishes. Leave the bottom of the cover open to prevent moisture buildup.

Bananas must be ripened off the plant, because the fruit will usually split if left on after maturity. Bananas also acquire most of their nutrients and sugars in the three to four weeks prior to maturity, however, so it is important not to pick too early. When hands at the top of the stalk begin to turn yellow, it's time to cut the entire stalk.

A mature stalk of bananas can be stored at 55° F for one to two weeks. Temperatures below 50° F will injure the fruit, so don't put them in the refrigerator. The fruit will ripen in several days at room temperature.

Bananas at the Table

Bananas are a favorite for fresh eating. You'll be amazed at how flavorful home-grown bananas can be. They are excellent in fruit salads, pies, cakes, and breads, and with ice cream.

Next time you have a barbecue, try grilling bananas for dessert. You can grill the whole fruit with the peel slit along the top. They will be especially delicious if basted with coconut milk or honey.

Bananas are also a popular addition to sandwich spreads. One favorite sandwich spread is a mixture of chopped chicken, pineapple, celery, bananas, and mayonnaise. Sliced bananas are delicious on sandwiches with peanut butter and raisins.

Plaintains must be cooked before eating and are often served hot as a starchy vegetable rather than a dessert. The usual method is to slice the fruit and simmer it in a frying pan with butter, sugar, and lemon juice until soft. Green bananas can also be cooked this way.

Special Pink Banana Butter
Pink banana butter is especially delicious on warm biscuits or muffins and makes a delightful filling for cakes.

    3½ pounds ripe bananas, mashed
        (10 small bananas; 4 cups
        mashed fruit)
     1 cup fresh or frozen
        raspberries
     ½ cup fresh lemon juice
     3 cups sugar
     1 teaspoon butter

Place all ingredients in a large pot and bring to a hard, rolling boil, stirring constantly. Reduce heat and simmer, stirring occasionally, for 20 minutes. Pour into hot, sterilized half-pint canning jars and seal with two-piece lids. Process in a boiling water bath for 15 minutes.

Makes 5 to 6 cups.

Left: Wee fingers point downward under the brilliant purple bracts of this banana flower. The male flowers are borne at the end of the stalk after the last hand of female flowers emerges. Right: As they mature, banana fruit curl upward to form the familiar "hands" of fruit. The tip of the stalk (containing the male flowers) has been removed.

Apple-Banana Bread

This recipe makes nicely shaped, moist loaves. Serve them warm from the oven, or cut the cooled bread in thick slices, and toast in a hot oven or toaster oven until golden.

- 4 eggs
- 2 cups sugar
- 1 cup butter or margarine, softened, cut into pats
- 1 cup chunky applesauce
- 1 cup diced banana (2 medium)
- ⅔ cup sour milk (see Note)
- 2 teaspoons vanilla extract
- 4 cups flour
- 2 teaspoons baking soda
- 1 teaspoon salt

1. Preheat oven to 350° F. In large bowl of electric mixer, mix eggs, sugar, butter, applesauce, banana, sour milk, and vanilla at low speed. In a separate bowl, combine flour, baking soda, and salt. Stir dry ingredients into the fruit mixture.

2. Grease and flour 4 small loaf pans (7½ by 3⅞ by 2¼ inches). Divide mixture among prepared pans. Bake until a toothpick inserted in center comes out clean, about 1 hour.

Makes 4 small loaves.

Note: To make sour milk, add 1½ tablespoons vinegar to ⅔ cup milk.

Tropical Banana Sorbet

This sorbet is low in fat and cholesterol. The banana flavor is more pronounced when passion fruit–orange nectar is used rather than lemon juice, but both are delicious.

- 2 cups water
- 1½ cups sugar
- 2 pounds (6 medium) bananas, peeled and sliced
- 1 cup orange juice
- ⅔ cup passion fruit–orange nectar or lemon juice

In a small saucepan combine water and sugar. Bring to a boil and boil 3 minutes to make syrup. Let cool. Combine syrup with banana and juices and purée in batches in an electric blender or food processor. Place mixture into canister of ice cream freezer and freeze according to manufacturer's instructions.

Makes 6 cups.

Cherimoya

Cherimoyas usually elicit a two-stage response from someone experiencing them for the first time—amazement and then delight. The amazement is sparked by the unusual appearance of the fruit. Cherimoyas look something like an artichoke crossed with a pineapple: They are large and heart-shaped with a thick green skin that looks as if it's made of overlapping scales. The delight is a reaction to the flavor of the fruit. Cherimoyas have a wonderful custardy texture and delicious tropical flavor with overtones of pineapple, banana, and papaya. Indeed, Mark Twain described the flavor as "deliciousness itself."

Overall, the cherimoya is an attractive tree. The leaves are about

Common Name: Cherimoya
Botanical Name: *Annona cherimola.*
Origin: Mountain valleys of Peru and Ecuador.
Growth Habit: Briefly deciduous tree or large shrub, 15 to 25 feet high by 15 to 20 feet wide.
Adaptation: Hardy to 29° F. Best adapted to the cooler, dry-summer climates of Southern California. Also grown in Hawaii.
Harvest Season: February through April.
Begins Bearing: Within 2 to 5 years after planting.
Propagation: Seedlings produce fruit of variable quality. Named varieties are cleft-grafted to two-year-old seedling rootstocks during the dormant season, just prior to bud break. Can also be shield-budded.
Maintenance: Moderate.
Pollination: Hand-pollination is usually required. See "Pollination" on page 24.
Suitability for Containers: Suitable only for large containers.
Landscape Quality: Attractive leaves but not very versatile.
Nurseries: E, I, O, P, Q, S, U, Y.
Information: 1, 2, 13, 14.

10 inches long by 4 inches wide, dull green on top and velvety green on the bottom. The tree is briefly deciduous in spring. It can be pruned as a spreading, multi-trunked tree 15 to 20 feet high or as an erect tree growing 25 feet high. Some growers have successfully pollarded (headed) the tree to a short trunk between 24 and 30 inches high. This severe pruning limits flowering to the new growth. Also, fewer flowers may be produced and the flowering may be delayed, but the lower plant profile makes hand-pollination much easier.

Adaptation

Cherimoyas grow best in areas with moderately warm summers and low relative humidity where winter temperatures drop below 45° F but not below freezing. Optimum summer temperatures range between 70° and 85° F, but the trees will produce in warmer areas. Winters should provide some chilling but be relatively frost free, because the fruit hangs on the tree through the cold months and will be damaged by freezing temperatures. The tree will tolerate brief periods of temperatures as low as 29° F. Prolonged exposure to subfreezing temperatures will cause serious dieback. If cherimoyas do not receive enough chilling, trees will go dormant slowly and then experience delayed foliation. The exact amount of chilling has not been

In the mountain valleys of Peru and Ecuador, the cherimoya is pollinated by a species of insect. In the United States, however, the flowers must be pollinated by hand.

determined, but is estimated to be between 50 and 100 hours of temperatures between 32° and 45° F.

Southern California provides the best conditions for growing cherimoyas in the United States. The largest commercial plantings are located slightly inland from the Pacific Ocean near Santa Barbara. Some varieties perform better in coastal or inland areas; these are noted on the variety charts. Cherimoyas do not adapt well to the tropical lowlands of Florida and Hawaii. The atemoya (see "Cherimoya Relatives" on page 25) is a better choice.

Pollination

The cherimoya flower is perfect, meaning it contains both male and female parts, but self-pollination usually doesn't take place, because the female flower part (the stigma) is receptive only on the day before the pollen is released. In areas where the plant is native, a species of insect spreads the pollen at the appropriate times. This insect isn't found in the United States, however, so you will have to pollinate the

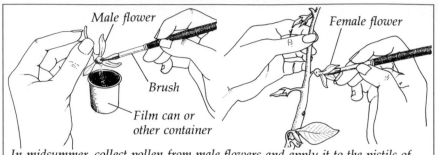

In midsummer, collect pollen from male flowers and apply it to the pistils of partially open female flowers. Repeat every few days during bloom.

flowers by hand to ensure fruit production. The plants flower over a long period in midsummer, so if you pollinate every couple of days during bloom the harvest period will extend over several months the following spring.

Sometimes the flowers self-pollinate when warm temperatures cause the pollen to mature early or when high humidity prolongs the receptiveness of the stigma. For this reason, trees in the humid coastal areas of California set more self-pollinated fruit than those in the drier interior valleys. Some gardeners in drier parts of the Southwest use fogging systems to raise the

humidity around the blooming trees; this increases self-pollination, but it is usually better to pollinate the flowers yourself if you want well-formed fruit. Self-pollinated fruit tend to be misshapen because not all the seeds develop.

Left: *Cherimoya:* Annona cherimola *'White'*

Below: *The cherimoya has handsome branchlets with leaves arranged in two opposite rows along the stem.*

Bottom: *Cherimoya:* Annona cherimola *'Spain'*

Some selected varieties seem to have a higher percentage of self-pollination, but their performance varies from area to area.

Site Selection and Planting

Cherimoyas prefer full sun and a deep, well-drained soil. The ideal soil pH is between 6 and 7.

Caring for Cherimoya Trees

Watering   Cherimoyas need plenty of moisture while they are growing actively, but should not be watered when they are dormant. The trees are susceptible to root rot in soggy soils, especially in cool weather. Drought-stressed trees will drop their leaves, exposing the fruit to sunburn.

Fertilizing   Fertilize cherimoyas on a regular basis. Apply about 2 ounces of a balanced fertilizer, such as 8-8-8, to young trees each month during the growing season up until midsummer or late summer. Increase the applications by an ounce each year until the trees begin to bear fruit. Mature trees should receive a pound of 8-8-8 fertilizer per inch of trunk diameter (measured at chest level).

Pruning   Cherimoyas have rather brittle wood. Prune during the dormant period to develop strong branches that can support the heavy fruit. When pruning, select branches with wide angles between the limb or trunk from which they originate. These branches are more strongly attached than those with narrow angles. Also, prune to encourage new growth and fruiting near the center of the tree, where the fruit will be protected from sunburn and birds. Also, fruit at the outside of the tree can bend branches to the ground, causing the fruit to become dirty and bruised.

Pests and Diseases   Few troublesome problems under good growing conditions. Nematodes can be a problem in older trees.

Harvest and Storage

Cherimoyas develop a pale green to creamy yellow color as they reach maturity. They should be picked when still firm and allowed to soften at room temperature. Ripe fruit will give to soft pressure. Overripe fruit will be dark brown. Fruit left on the tree too long will usually crack or split and begin to decay. You'll probably have to harvest fruit every couple of days if you pollinated over an extended period. The fruit should be clipped, rather than pulled, from the tree. Cut the stem close to the fruit so it won't puncture other fruit during storage.

Store mature fruit above 55° F to prevent chilling injury to the skin and flesh. Ripe fruit will deteriorate quickly but can be stored at temperatures lower than 55° F for short periods, although they may become discolored. Ripe cherimoyas can be frozen, and eaten like ice cream.

Cherimoya Relatives

Many close relatives of the cherimoya also produce delicious fruit. Some of the best are described in the following paragraphs.

The sweetsop or sugar apple, *Annona squamosa*, is very similar to the cherimoya but is better adapted to Florida. The fruit are noticeably knobbier than the cherimoya and the trees are slightly smaller, rarely exceeding 15 feet high. The sweetsop is not hardy below 29° F. Most are grown from seed.

The atemoya is a hybrid of the cherimoya and the sweetsop. It combines the hardiness of the cherimoya with the sweetsop's tolerance of warm, humid climates. It is most widely planted in Florida. There are many varieties available, some of which are still being evaluated. The variety 'Gefner' reliably produces good fruit without hand-pollination.

Another cherimoya relative, the soursop (*Annona muricata*) has fruit covered with long, curved, fleshy spines. The trees are upright and may reach 20 feet high and 15 feet wide. Less hardy than the sweetsop, the soursop will usually be damaged if the temperature drops below 30° F. Seedling-grown trees are not reliable producers of quality fruit. The most readily available selected soursop variety is called 'Fiberless Cuban'.

Cherimoyas at the Table

Cherimoyas are best served chilled, cut in half or quartered, and eaten with a spoon. Adding anything to the fruit is likely to mask its wonderful fragrance and encumber its delicious tropical flavor. The fruit can also be juiced or used to make delicious sorbets or milkshakes.

Cherimoya Varieties

VARIETY	FRUIT CHARACTERISTICS	COMMENTS
Bays	Medium, skin smooth, yellow-green. Very good, lemon flavor. Ripens December to April.	Spreading tree, well adapted to coastal areas.
Booth	Small to medium, skin slightly knobby, yellowish green. Conical shape. Papaya flavor. Ripens November to March.	Partially self-pollinating in coastal areas. Fruit has many seeds.
Chaffey	Small to medium, skin smooth, thick. Rich, lemon flavor. Ripens January to April.	Tree has open habit. Thick skin on fruit resists bruises.
Deliciosa	Medium, skin prickly. Very good flavor.	
El Bumpo	Medium, skin very prickly. Excellent flavor. Ripens December to March.	
Honeyhart	Medium, skin smooth, plated, yellowish green. Pulp has smooth texture, excellent flavor. Ripens November to March.	Very juicy.
Mariella	Medium, skin knobby, yellowish green. Very good flavor. Ripens November to March.	Similar to White.
Ott	Small to medium, skin thick with smooth, heart-shaped plates. Excellent pineapple-banana flavor. Ripens January to April.	Resists bruising.
Pierce	Small to large, skin knobby, light green. Very sweet, pineapple-banana flavor. Ripens January to March.	Partially self-pollinating. Has a tendency toward alternate bearing. Few seeds.
Spain	Small to large, skin smooth, dark green. Cone-shaped. Good banana flavor. Ripens December to April.	Partially self-fruitful in coastal areas.
Villa Park	Small to medium, round, skin has small bumps. Sweet, pineapple-banana flavor. Ripens December to March.	
White	Small to medium, skin rough. Sweet, papaya-mango flavor. Ripens December to March.	Good along the California coast. Open tree.

Citrus

Tracing the migration and development of citrus fruit is like taking a course in world history. Citrus were used as medicinals in ancient India and in the empires of the Medes and the Persians; they were pampered in the orangeries of Louis XIV at Versailles, and, after being introduced into the New World by Christopher Columbus, savored by Americans as their most important fruit crop.

Today citrus plants are some of the most rewarding for the home gardener. Consider their qualities: lustrous, emerald-green foliage, sweetly perfumed white blossoms, and, of course, brightly colored fruit that hang like jewels from the branches. Even types of citrus that are usually considered inedible, such as sour oranges, are widely used as ornamentals.

Citrus also offer great variety. Mature plants range in size from small shrubs, such as the 'Meyer' lemon, to large trees, such as the vigorously growing grapefruit.

Leaves range from the small, pointed foliage of the 'Chinotto' orange to the large, lush, tropical-looking leaves of the pummelo.

The fruit can be as small as beans on the kumquat, or almost as large as basketballs on the pummelo.

The fruit color may be the pale yellow of lemons, citrons, and pummelos, the bright orange of the sweet orange varieties, or the brilliant red-orange of such fruit as the 'Temple' orange, 'Dancy' mandarin, and 'Minneola' tangelo.

The colors of the flesh and juice of citrus fruits are as variable as the colors of the outer rinds. Lemons and limes have pale yellowish green flesh and juice. The most brilliantly colored juice comes from the 'Moro' blood orange and the 'Star Ruby' grapefruit.

The myriad flavors of citrus fruits is unmatched by any other type of fruit. One can choose among the highly acidic and aromatic flavors of lemons and limes; the tangy, spicy flavors of the mandarins; the sprightly sweet flavor of the oranges; the sweet, rich, almost syrupy flavor of the 'Kinnow' mandarin; and the aromatic flavor and perfumed bouquet of the 'Chandler' pummelo. Even the bitter flavor of the sour oranges is esteemed by connoisseurs of marmalades and bitters.

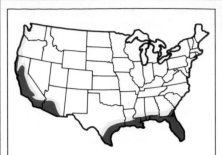

Common Name: Citrus.

Botanical Name: Most common types are species of *Citrus* or *Fortunella*.

Origin: The progenitors of most citrus originated in the Malay–East Indonesian Archipelago over 20 million years ago. Modern varieties come from all over the world.

Growth Habit: Varies by species and variety. Most are evergreen shrubs or trees from 2 to more than 20 feet tall.

Adaptation: The primary areas of outdoor culture are in California valleys, California and Arizona low deserts, Texas, the Gulf Coast, and Florida. Exact hardiness and adaptation differs according to type and variety.

Harvest Season: Depends on variety and growing area. Primary season begins in late October and extends through April, but some citrus is available throughout the year.

Begins Bearing: Usually within 3 to 4 years for grafted trees. Full production in 7 to 8 years for standard trees.

Propagation: Seedlings often have unpredictable fruit quality. Selected varieties are usually budded or grafted to specific rootstocks. Can also be grown from cuttings.

Maintenance: Low.

Pollination: Most varieties are self-fruitful.

Suitability for Containers: Excellent, especially dwarfs.

Landscape Quality: Excellent.

Nurseries: A, B, C, I, F, M, O, P, Q, U, Y.

Information: 1, 2, 3, 8, 9, 13, 14.

Left: *Under favorable conditions 'Bearss' limes flower and set fruit throughout the year.*

Opposite: *Citrus sizes (from largest to smallest): 'Chandler' pummelo, 'Star Ruby' grapefruit, 'Minneola' tangelo, 'Robertson' navel, 'Valencia' orange, 'Moro' blood orange, 'Dancy' mandarin, 'Eureka' lemon, 'Bearss' lime, 'Chinotto' sour orange, 'Rangpur' lime, 'Nagami' kumquat, 'Golden Bean' kumquat.*

Before Western civilization discovered the edible sweet orange, citrus were grown in orangeries for the fragrance of the flowers and peel. Louis XIV grew citrus not for the fruit but so his stately banquets could be blessed with the fragrance of the blossoms. The rind of the bergamot (*Citrus bergamia*) is still used to make eau de cologne, the most widely used of toilet waters, and is an important ingredient in many other perfume products.

Adaptation

It's hard to imagine a fruit more drastically affected by climate variations than citrus.

Seasonal temperature variations have the most important influence on adaptation. The lowest temperature at which growth takes place is 55° F; The highest is approximately 100° F. The optimum temperature for growth of oranges ranges between 70° and 90° F. There are, of course, some differences between varieties and species.

Hardiness differs according to species, and sometimes variety, of citrus. Trees can usually withstand temperatures 3 to 4 degrees lower than those that will damage the fruit. Also, ripe fruit can withstand lower temperatures than can immature or green fruit. For this reason gardeners in marginal citrus areas select early-maturing varieties, which usually ripen before the first frost. Fully dormant 'Satsuma' mandarin trees can withstand temperatures as low as 18° F without defoliation. Kumquats may tolerate temperatures a degree or two colder. Most other mandarins can take 22° to 23° F; grapefruit and oranges 23° to 24° F; lemons 26° to 27° F; and limes 28° F. The average freezing point for mature fruits of 'Satsuma' mandarins and 'Temple' tangors is 28° F. Ripe navel oranges freeze at 27° to 28° F. Half-ripe navel orange fruit is damaged at 28° to 29° F.

Duration of cold is also very important in determining whether fruit will be damaged. It usually takes 3 or 4 hours at 27° to 28° F to injure navel oranges, but it may take only 30 to 60 minutes at 29° F to injure small lemons.

Citrus also have heat requirements. All varieties of grapefruit require long, hot growing seasons to reach peak quality and sweetness. They are best adapted to Texas, Florida, and low-elevation desert areas of Arizona and California. Other types of citrus have lower heat requirements and can be grown in cooler areas. Lemons probably have the lowest heat requirement and can be grown in the cool coastal areas of California.

The citrus varieties described in the Citrus Varieties Charts on pages 41 to 43 are recommended according to the following areas:

California

This large area includes both the northern and the southern parts of the state. Summers are usually hot and dry; most rain falls in the winter. Southern California, with its many frost-free microclimates, is a traditional citrus area. In the inland valleys of Southern California almost any citrus can be grown. Northern California also has frost-free areas, but along the coast the summers are too cool for many varieties. Winters are cool and rainy. Many more types of citrus are adapted to the inland areas of Northern California, where there is more summer heat but also a greater chance of cold winters.

California and Arizona Deserts

These low-elevation areas have extremely hot summers, warm winters, strong sunlight, and gusty winds. Varieties with high heat requirements are best here, but sunburn and wind damage are very common.

Texas and the Gulf Coast

These areas are usually hot and humid with some rainfall the year around. Western Texas is drier and warmer; some areas resemble desert climates. Cold waves of Arctic air are common in the winter, so select hardy, early varieties that will ripen before winter.

Florida

This hot, humid region has many frost-free areas, although occasionally a freeze will devastate citrus throughout the state. Rainfall is spread throughout the year.

Climate Effects

Climate has a strong influence on fruit size, shape, flavor, and juice content, as well as the color, texture, and thickness of the peel. Climate also affects the rate of growth, habit, and flowering of the trees. In general, climate influences citrus in the following ways:

Bloom

Trees flower earliest in hot, humid areas and latest in cool, semiarid coastal areas. Thus 'Valencia' oranges reach peak bloom in mid-March in Orlando, Florida and Weslaco, Texas; early April in the hot desert areas of Arizona and California; and early May in the cool coastal valleys of Southern California.

Maturity

Fruit grown in a hot area ripens before fruit of the same variety grown in a cooler area. This is because there is a close (but not absolute) relationship between the accumulated heat units in a growing season (the heat accumulation) and date of maturity. A heat unit index is calculated by adding together all of the mean daily temperatures greater than 55° F between bloom and maturity.

'Valencia' oranges ripen in February in the hot, humid climates of Florida and Texas and the hot, arid climates of California and Arizona deserts. In cool coastal areas of California, 'Valencia' may not ripen until June.

Fruit Size

Fruit is usually largest in hot, humid climates, becoming progressively smaller in hot, arid climates and cool, arid climates. Varieties that produce large fruit in arid, subtropical areas of California sometimes produce fruit that is too large when grown in Florida. Likewise, varieties such as 'Hamlin' and 'Pineapple', which reach marketable size in Florida, are too small for commercial acceptance when grown in California.

Fruit Shape

Fruit tends to be longer in relation to width in hotter areas and flatter in cooler climates.

Peel Characteristics

Peels are thin and smooth in hot, humid Florida and Texas. In arid regions of the West, they are thicker with a rougher texture.

Color Development

In truly tropical areas citrus remain green when ripe. In hot, humid areas of Florida and Texas, rind color remains pale in most varieties. The most intense color develops in arid climates of the West, where low temperatures prevail for several weeks before harvest.

Citrus shapes (above) and cross sections (opposite): 1. 'Golden Bean' kumquat 2. 'Sinton' citrangequat 3. 'Eustis' limequat 4. 'Meiwa' kumquat 5. 'Nagami' kumquat 6. 'Calamondin' mandarin 7. 'Moro' blood orange 8. 'Tarocco' blood orange 9. 'Lisbon' lemon 10. 'Eureka' lemon 11. 'Improved Meyer' lemon 12. 'Kusai' lime 13. 'Rangpur' lime 14. 'Bearss' lime 15. 'Mexican' lime 16. 'Orlando' tangelo 17. 'Minneola' tangelo 18. 'Dancy' mandarin 19. 'Clementine' mandarin 20. 'Satsuma' mandarin

The red color of the flesh and rind of blood oranges is due to the presence of the pigment anthocyanin. This pigment develops best in warm, intermediate climates, such as those in the interior valleys of Central and Southern California. Red coloration is less intense in the hot desert areas of the Southwest. In humid climates, blood oranges rarely turn red.

The red color in grapefruit and pummelos is produced by a different pigment—lycopene. In this case, strong coloration is directly related to high temperatures during maturation. Thus, red varieties of grapefruit and pummelos develop their most intense color in hot climates. Grapefruit and pummelos develop little or no red color in cool climates.

Juice Content
Citrus fruits are juiciest when grown in hot, humid climates and less juicy in regions that are hot and arid or cool and humid.

Flavor
Sugar and acid are the main components of citrus flavor that are influenced by climate. Fruit grown in arid climates that have a cold period before the fruit matures tends to have more acid and a better balance between sugars and acids than those grown in humid climates. This usually means the fruit from the arid areas have a richer flavor, although many people prefer the sweeter taste common to fruit grown in humid areas. Overall, the percentage of acid in the juice is higher in fruit grown in cooler climates.

Tree Habit
Trees grow fastest in hot, humid climates and slowest in cooler areas. As a result, trees in colder climates are usually more compact.

When all these effects are combined, the result is that a variety grown in the Southeast is lighter in color, has a thinner rind, is juicier, and tastes sweeter than the same variety grown in the West. This is the main reason why the more colorful, richer-flavored, commercially grown California oranges are usually sold fresh, and Florida oranges are made into juice.

Pollination
Most varieties are self-fruitful, but some varieties produce more fruit when pollinated by another variety. This need for cross-pollination is noted in the "Comments" sections of the variety charts.

Propagation
Most citrus trees are propagated by budding the desired variety to a specific type of rootstock. Budded trees are preferred over seedling trees because they are reliably true to type, come into production sooner, and benefit from desirable rootstock effects, such as disease resistance, greater cold tolerance, dwarfing, better fruit quality, early maturity, and adaptation to adverse soil conditions.

21. 'Honey' mandarin 22. 'Nova' mandarin 23. 'Fairchild' mandarin 24. 'Kara' mandarin 25. 'Chinotto' orange 26. 'Bouquet de Fleurs' sour orange 27. 'Seville' sour orange 28. 'Shamouti' orange 29. 'Valencia' orange 30. 'Pineapple' orange 31. 'Marrs' orange 32. 'Temple' tangor 33. 'Washington' navel 34. 'Robertson' navel 35. 'Redblush' grapefruit 36. 'Star Ruby' grapefruit 37. 'Oroblanco' grapefruit 38. 'Marsh' grapefruit 39. 'Chandler' pummelo 40. 'Etrog' citron 41. 'Buddha's Hand' citron.

Citrus seeds will often produce two or more seedlings, a result of a phenomenon known as *nucellar embryony*. One of these seedlings is the result of pollination and will produce a tree that will have characteristics of both parents. The others, which are not the result of pollination, are *nucellar seedlings*, which are identical to the tree from which they came. Different varieties of citrus produce nucellar seedlings at different rates. Varieties that produce a large percentage of nucellar seedlings can be grown from seed because the seedling tree will be identical to the parent. Nucellar seedlings are often used as citrus rootstocks.

Fresh citrus seeds will germinate easily at soil temperatures between 80° and 90° F. They lose their viability rapidly when allowed to dry out. To store citrus seeds, pack them in moist (not wet) peat moss and keep them in the refrigerator for up to six months.

Rootstocks

'Troyer' and 'Carrizo' citranges are the best rootstocks for standard-sized oranges, grapefruits, mandarins, tangelos, and 'Lisbon' lemons. They are resistant to several crown and root diseases and produce excellent-quality fruit. Rough lemon and *Citrus macrophylla* are the best rootstocks for 'Eureka' lemons and 'Persian' limes.

Trifoliate orange *(Poncirus trifoliata)* is the most common dwarfing rootstock. It is also disease resistant and causes fruit to ripen slightly earlier. More importantly, it is also more cold tolerant than the other rootstocks and thus is highly recommended in cold climates. Trifoliate orange will dwarf most varieties by 30 to 50 percent in home garden conditions. The trifoliate variety 'Flying Dragon' provides even more dwarfing; trees on this rootstock will not grow much taller than 5 to 6 feet high.

Site Selection and Planting

Citrus trees are usually sold in containers but are sometimes sold balled and burlapped. Trees purchased by mail may be shipped bare root. The best time to plant is in early spring, after the danger of frost has passed. For best results the soil pH should be between 6 and 7.

All citrus trees prefer maximum exposure to sunlight, but in desert climates some light shade during the hottest part of the day may prevent sunburned fruit. In cool climates, plant in the warmest possible microclimate, such as against a light-colored, south-facing wall.

Caring For Citrus

Most citrus are easy to care for, requiring minimal pruning and infrequent pest control. All they usually need is regular watering and fertilization.

Watering   Citrus trees need adequate soil moisture for healthy growth and good fruit production. Drought during bloom causes the flowers to drop and results in poor fruit set. Lack of moisture during the growing season causes fruit drop and low yields. Prolonged drought will defoliate and eventually kill the tree. At the other extreme, standing water and poorly drained soils are almost always lethal to citrus trees. Plant in well-drained soil, and water citrus regularly during dry periods.

Fertilizing   Citrus trees need to be fertilized regularly. The number of applications depends on the region; consult the chart on page 31 for timing and rates.

Soils in some areas will also be deficient in micronutrients. In these cases the trees will need foliar sprays of micronutrients.

Pruning   Citrus trees do not require regular pruning to remain productive and are usually allowed to develop on their own. You may, however, want to prune to control the size of lemons and other vigorous types. Most citrus can also be sheared regularly as a hedge or trained as an espalier and still produce some fruit.

Very old, overgrown trees can be rejuvenated by severe pruning. Known as skeletonizing, this radical pruning method involves removing all limbs greater than 1 to 2 inches in diameter. If you are going to skeletonize a tree, do so in early spring so it can regrow during the following growing season. The tree won't produce any fruit for about 2 years, but when it does begin to bear again, the fruit will usually will be larger than normal. Skeletonizing is effective only on otherwise healthy trees—it is not a cure for diseases.

The bark of citrus trees is very susceptible to sunburn, especially after severe pruning. Always paint exposed branches and trunks with diluted (50-50) water-based white paint or commercially available whitewash after heavy pruning.

Pests and Diseases   Vigorously growing trees have few problems,

Citrus trees respond well to pruning. Vigorous species, such as these lemon trees, can be trained over arbors.

Fertilizing Young Citrus Trees

In clay soils of the West, usually only nitrogen is required. In the Southeast, use a balanced fertilizer containing micronutrients.

California, Arizona, and Texas

Years after Planting	Number of Applications per year (February to September)	Pounds of actual Nitrogen per application*
1	3	0.1
2	3	0.2
3	2	0.4
4	2	0.45
5	2	0.5
6	2	0.55
7	2	0.6
8-10 (mature)	2	0.6-0.75

Florida and the Gulf Coast

1	4 to 5	0.1
2	4	0.2
3	3	0.3
4	3	0.4
5	3	0.45
6	3	0.45-0.5
7-10 (mature)	3	0.5

*See page 80 for an example calculation of the pounds of actual nitrogen in a fertilizer.

but even robust trees occasionally become infested with mites, scale, thrips, or whiteflies. Trees in poorly drained soils often succumb to various diseases and cankers of the roots or trunk.

Harvest and Storage

Citrus fruits mature at various times of the year. Early varieties of oranges and mandarins ripen in October or November of the year in which they bloomed. Late varieties of orange, mandarin, and grapefruit mature from February to May. In hot, humid regions, such as Florida and Texas, the fruits mature slightly before the same varieties grown in the hot, dry desert regions of the Southwest and well before fruit in the cool coastal areas of California.

In California, 'Washington' navel and 'Valencia' oranges are grown in three distinct climate areas—cool, intermediate, and hot. As a result, California growers harvest fresh oranges throughout the year. The navels mature in November in the warmest areas, but may be picked as late as June in cooler

Citrus trees may be sheared for a formal effect, as with this orange tree at Hearst Castle in California.

areas. The 'Valencia' oranges begin to mature in February in desert areas and, in cooler climates, the harvest extends into October.

The only sure way to determine maturity is to taste the fruit. Fruit color is a poor indication of ripeness, because many fruits have fully colored rinds months before they can be eaten. Lemons, limes, and other acid citrus are an exception. They can be picked whenever they reach acceptable size and juice content.

Once mature, most citrus fruits can be stored on the tree for several weeks and picked as needed. Mandarins are an exception, holding their fruit for shorter periods than oranges, grapefruits, or lemons. When mandarins have been on the tree too long, they lose their juice and the pulp dries out. A puffy rind is another indication that the fruit is overly mature.

Most citrus fruits can also be stored in the refrigerator for at least two to three weeks. Under dry conditions at room temperature, fruits develop "off" flavors, wither, and become unattractive within a week to 10 days.

Types of Citrus

Citron

Citrons (*Citrus medica*) are large, thick-skinned fruit resembling lemons. The trees are scraggly and very frost sensitive, but the plants are sometimes grown as a novelty or for the ceremonies associated with the Jewish Feast of Tabernacles.

'Etrog' is the most commonly planted variety, but the fingered citron, or 'Buddha's Hand,' has a more unusual shape.

Citrons at the Table

The citron resembles the lemon in its cooking characteristics, with one important difference: The pulpy flesh of the citron yields little or no juice. Thus, only the thick rind of the citron is used—candied, for flavoring, and in marmalades. In fact, many Americans have only seen the candied and dyed citron rind, sold for use in fruitcakes and Christmas puddings.

The fingered citron ('Buddha's Hand') is an ornamental. In a pinch its "fingers" may be grated and used for flavoring, but the tentacles of this unusual fruit are mostly pith (the zest would be almost impossible to separate) and there are many fruits that are better for preserves.

Grapefruit

Grapefruits appear to have originated in the West Indies. Researchers believe they are natural hybrids of the pummelo, but the exact parentage is unknown.

Grapefruits are borne on large trees with big, deep green leaves. They require a long, hot growing season to reach peak quality, but their ability to hang on the tree for long periods without deteriorating allows them to attain acceptable flavor in cooler areas.

There are two types of fruit: white fleshed and pigmented. 'Duncan' and 'Marsh Seedless' have white flesh, while 'Ruby', 'Redblush', and 'Star Ruby' develop pink to red flesh and a reddish rind in hot climates. Pigmented grapefruit doesn't color well in cool climates.

'Oroblanco' is a recently introduced grapefruit-pummelo hybrid developed by the University of California. It bears incredibly juicy fruit with a sweet, low-acid flavor.

Grapefruit at the Table

Although grapefruits are commonplace and available nearly the year around now, they are still often considered an elegant treat, perhaps because they were so rare until as recently as the beginning of this century. In salads, the grapefruit is as versatile as the orange, though its tartness necessitates a different treatment. Sections of grapefruit can be arranged on a plate with greens as bitter as watercress, but their tartness should be offset by one of the sweet vinegars (balsamic, raspberry, or a good cider vinegar) and a fruity olive or walnut oil. Consider adding nonbitter vegetables, such as parboiled artichoke hearts or roasted sweet red peppers or even bits of sweet fruit such as dried dates to a grapefruit salad. Avocados and grapefruit are a classic combination.

There is basically no flavor difference between pink and white grapefruit, but there is a difference between seedy and seedless fruit. Seedy fruits have a richer, more pronounced flavor and separate into segments easily. For this reason they are often grown for commercial processing. If you want the best-flavored juice, consider growing 'Duncan', a seedy variety.

Cooked and sweetened with sugar, grapefruit makes excellent marmalade and candied peel. Take advantage of a prolific harvest by making freshly squeezed, chilled grapefruit juice and serving it at

Above: *The fingered, or 'Buddha's Hand' citron has the most unusual shape of any citrus.*

Right: *'Star Ruby' grapefruit is a seedless variety with deep-red flesh.*

brunches. Or make a fancy grapefruit sorbet and serve it as a palate cleanser or with delicate wafers as a light dessert.

Choose grapefruits that are heavy (indicating a high percentage of juice) and thin skinned. Ignore superficial scars and russetting; they have no effect on quality.

Kumquats and Their Hybrids

Kumquats are hardy species of *Fortunella*. They are good-looking trees densely covered with small leaves. They can get quite large on vigorous rootstocks, but are usually small and compact—ideal for containers.

Because of their hardiness (to at least 18° F), kumquats have been used for hybridization with other species of citrus, such as limes (limequats) and oranges (orangequats). Both limequats and orangequats are very ornamental plants.

Kumquats and Their Hybrids at the Table

Kumquats are usually preserved and used whole as garnishes for meats or made into marmalade. They are, however, also delightful when eaten fresh: Just roll and squeeze the fruit between your fingers to combine the sweet flavors of the skin with the tart flavors of the pulp. The hybrids of the kumquat range in sweetness; the orangequat is the sweetest (sweeter than the kumquat) and the limequat is very tart. Limequats can be substituted for limes in cooking.

Kumquats can be found in grocery stores from November through the spring. Their size and seediness depends on maturity at harvest time and on the variety, but all are edible out-of-hand.

In addition to their culinary value, kumquats are also very decorative and are often used as holiday season table centerpieces, their bright orange skins contrasting with a few bright green leaves left on their stems. Kumquat hybrids also make attractive table decorations; the orangequat is a little larger than the kumquat and bright orange; the limequat is smaller and bright yellow.

Because of the kumquat's diminutive size, which permits it to be used halved, and because it is quite tart and pungent, it is excellent in sauces for rich meats such as duck, goose, pork, or even lamb. The following recipe makes an elegant traditional French sauce for duckling.

Roast Duck With Kumquat Sauce

1 duckling (4½ to 5 lbs)
Pepper
2 yellow onions
¼ teaspoon dried thyme
16 kumquats
¼ cup olive oil
4 cups chicken stock, preferably homemade
2 bay leaves
Black peppercorns
Half a bunch parsley (2 cups, packed)
¼ cup red wine vinegar
2 tablespoons sugar
2 tablespoons Marsala or sherry
1 tablespoon cornstarch

1. Preheat oven to 450° F. Wash the duckling and dry it thoroughly. Reserve the giblets. Remove excess fat from around both cavities. Pierce the bird all over with a fork. Sprinkle the bird inside and out with pepper.

2. Quarter 1 of the onions and put into duckling's body cavity with the thyme and 2 of the kumquats, halved. Tie drumsticks together.

3. Put the bird breast side up in a high-sided baking pan (to prevent

Left: *Kumquat:* Fortunella margarita 'Nagami'

Above: 'Eustis' limequat, a lime-kumquat hybrid

spattering in the oven), and bake for 20 minutes.

4. Reduce oven to 350° F and continue to bake for another hour. Check for doneness by piercing at the leg joints. If the juices are pink, the meat will be underdone; clear juices indicate properly done meat.

5. While duckling is in the oven, slice the remaining onion. In a medium saucepan heat olive oil and sauté the giblets and onion until browned.

6. Slowly add chicken stock while scraping and incorporating the browned bits from the bottom of the pan.

7. Add bay leaves, a few peppercorns, and parsley and simmer until the stock is reduced by half. Strain. You should have 2 cups of brown stock.

8. In a small saucepan, boil the vinegar with the sugar until the mixture is slightly thickened. Slowly add the 2 cups strained stock, stirring and skimming off any fat that rises to the surface.

9. Thinly slice the remaining 14 kumquats, discarding seeds and stem ends; add them to the sauce. Simmer 10 minutes.

10. In a small bowl mix Marsala and cornstarch until smooth. Add to the sauce while stirring. Cook until thick and smooth. Add salt to taste. Keep sauce warm until the duck is ready.

11. Serve the duckling with sauce.

Serves 4.

Lemon

Lemon trees are among the most vigorous of the citrus family. Standard trees can reach over 20 feet high. They respond well to pruning, however, and are one of the few citrus trees that should be regularly cut back to keep them compact and the fruit within reach. Lemons are attractive plants with light green leaves that have a reddish tinge when young.

Lemons are best adapted to the western states, where fruits remain small and the trees are less likely to be infected with disease. In hot, humid climates, limes are preferred. In the coastal areas of California, lemon trees usually bear several crops a year. In warmer areas, lemons are picked from fall through winter. Harvest your lemons whenever they reach acceptable size and color.

The 'Meyer' lemon is not a true lemon but is a very popular lemon substitute. It was discovered near Peking, China, by Frank N. Meyer, a U.S.D.A. plant explorer, and was introduced to the United States in 1908. Since then its handsome, compact habit has made it one of the most popular dooryard citrus varieties. 'Meyer' lemons are productive for years in containers and can be trained to form a dense hedge. 'Improved Meyer' is a virus-free form that has replaced the original 'Meyer' clone.

Lemons at the Table

Having a bearing lemon tree can become as necessary to a cook as having a kitchen herb garden. A day hardly goes by that at least one lemon is not needed for a dish or refreshing drink. Lemon zest adds a sophisticated dimension to such diverse foods as stews, chocolate cake, and pizza. (Remember, when

Left: *Another formal design with citrus—a lemon allee, or walkway.*

Above: *Lemons often flower over a long period, providing a continuous supply of freshly ripened fruit. This is a 'Eureka' lemon.*

using the rind of any citrus fruit, that the fragrant, flavorful oils are in the thin, pigmented outer portion, or zest, of the peel. The inner, pithy portion can be bitter.) When your tree is producing too many lemons for you to consume or give away (or when lemons are particularly inexpensive at the greengrocer's), and you do not have the time to make lemon marmalade, squeeze the juice and freeze it in a freezer tray. A plastic bag full of lemon juice cubes is a bag of gold to the cook. Make hot toddies with them in the evening (boiled with water, brown sugar, and a clove, with rum added); use them in chicken, game, or pork marinades; make lemonade; or use them to make mayonnaise, Hollandaise sauce, or a simple mixture of juice and melted butter for vegetables.

When you serve a Tuscan, Provencal, Spanish, or other hearty Mediterranean stew or braised meat, have a little dish of *gremolata* on the table for guests to sprinkle on their meat. To make gremolata, mince 1 part lemon zest with 1 part garlic cloves and 2 parts parsley.

In this recipe for lemon pork, a lemon marinade and sauce adds a fresh, tangy flavor to the meat.

Lemon Pork, Southern Style

1 pork loin (3 lbs)
1 tablespoon Dijon mustard
Freshly ground black pepper
¼ cup lemon juice
½ cup bourbon
½ teaspoon salt
3 tablespoons light brown sugar
1 lemon, sliced paper-thin
3 tablespoons water

1. Pierce pork with a large fork, making deep holes for marinade to penetrate. Rub roast with mustard, grind pepper over it, and put it into a glass, stainless steel, or ceramic baking dish or bowl.

2. Combine lemon juice, bourbon and salt. Pour mixture over pork, cover with plastic wrap, and let it marinate at least 6 hours in the refrigerator. Turn pork in marinade several times.

3. Preheat oven to 350° F. Drain and reserve the marinade. Press the brown sugar onto the pork and insert a meat thermometer into the center. Roast pork for 1½ hours, basting occasionally with marinade. The roast is done when the meat thermometer reads 175° F.

4. Transfer pork to a carving board and cover with foil to keep warm.

5. Using a spatula, scrape the browned meat drippings from the bottom of the baking dish and transfer with juices and any reserved marinade to a small saucepan. Skim off excess fat if you like. Add the lemon slices and water and simmer until the lemon is tender, about 10 minutes.

6. Carve the meat and top with the lemon slices and sauce.

Serves 6.

Lime

Limes can be divided into two horticultural groups: the small-fruited 'Mexican', West Indian, or Key lime and the large-fruited Persian or 'Tahiti' lime. The 'Mexican' lime is the most important commercial variety and is often referred to as the bartender's lime. The deep green fruit

Above: *Two popular lemon varieties: 'Eureka' (top), and 'Lisbon' (bottom).*

Right: *'Mexican lime':* Citrus aurantiifolia

is borne on small, thorny trees that are very frost sensitive and best adapted to humid climates. Persian limes are grown commercially on a small scale in southern Florida and in a few places in Southern California. These trees are a few degrees hardier than the West Indian lime and have a more compact, attractive habit. The fruit is lighter green than West Indian but has a good lime flavor.

Both types of lime are harvested when they reach acceptable size. Fully mature fruit turns yellow.

The 'Rangpur' lime is actually an acid mandarin with small, juicy, bright orange fruit.

Limes at the Table

The West Indian (or Key) lime is the most aromatic of the limes and for that reason is preferred for marmalades, garnishes, and the famous Key lime pie. The "authentic" Key lime pie is the subject of much argument: It has been made a variety of ways, topped with a meringue or as a chiffon pie, with a short crust or with a crust made of crumbs. To make one, simply substitute Key lime zest and juice for lemon zest and juice in your favorite lemon pie recipe.

The juicy Persian lime is excellent for making limeade and marinades for meats. If sliced very thin, it can be eaten, rind and all, in many dishes, such as this elegant lime tart.

Lime Curd Tart

 1½ cups flour
  1 tablespoon sugar
     Pinch salt
 ½ cup butter
 ½ cup plus 1 tablespoon lime juice (5 to 7 limes)
  6 eggs
 ⅔ cup sugar
 10 tablespoons very cold, unsalted butter, cut into bits
  1 tablespoon grated lime rind
  1 lime, sliced paper-thin
  3 tablespoons grapefruit or lemon marmalade, melted and strained

1. Preheat oven to 450° F. Combine flour, 1 tablespoon sugar, and salt.

2. Cut in the ½ cup butter to get a crumbly texture that is very fine and slightly moist.

3. Turn mixture into a 9-inch flan or tart pan with removable bottom, and press gently with fingertips into an even tart shell.

4. Bake until light golden brown, 10 minutes. Remove pastry shell from oven; reduce heat to 400° F.

5. Combine lime juice, eggs, the ⅔ cup sugar, and the 10 tablespoons butter in top of a double boiler and set over simmering water. Cook, whisking constantly, until thick and smooth, about 10 minutes.

6. Strain mixture into a bowl and stir in the grated lime rind.

7. Pour the lime curd into the partially baked shell and bake at 400° F until the curd has softly set, about 30 minutes. Cool on a rack.

8. When tart is cool, arrange lime slices on top and brush with the marmalade.

Serves 8.

Mandarins and Their Hybrids

Mandarins offer great variety. Their fruit range from small to large, ripen early to late, and vary in color and flavor. The trees range from tall and upright to small and compact. Some have weeping habits. The foliage is hardier than that of an orange, but the fruit is not.

Mandarins are often called kid-

Top Left: 'Mexican' lime

Bottom Left: 'Rangpur' lime

Above: 'Bearss' lime

Top Right: 'Dancy' mandarin

Bottom Right: 'Minneola' tangelo

glove or loose-skin oranges because they are so easy to peel. Some brightly colored varieties are also known as tangerines.

If you choose your varieties carefully, you can harvest mandarins from November to April or May. The flavor of mandarins ranges from sprightly to sweet to almost spicy. The fruit won't hold on the tree as well as oranges, becoming puffy, dry, and insipid.

Some varieties of mandarin will set more fruit if pollinated by another variety planted nearby.

Tangelos Tangelos are hybrids of mandarins with grapefruits or pummelos. As you would expect from such a diverse group, the fruits vary tremendously. Colors range from pale yellow to deep orange. Sizes range from medium-small to medium-large, and the flavors are all quite distinctive, aromatic, and rich, often combining the best of both parents. Most varieties are best adapted to hot climates.

Tangors Tangors are hybrids between mandarins and oranges. 'Temple' and 'Murcott' are thought to be naturally occurring hybrids, although their exact parentage is unknown.

The fruit flavor varies between orange and mandarin, depending on the variety. The trees are about as hardy as orange trees and are slightly smaller. Tangors are best adapted to Florida.

Mandarins and Their Hybrids at the Table

It's difficult to generalize about the eating characteristics of mandarins, tangelos, and tangors. They range from very sweet to tart; some are seedless and some are full of seeds; some are fairly large while others are tiny. They do, however, share an ease of peeling and sectioning and, most importantly, the distinctive mandarin flavor, which is strong in some mandarins and quite subtle in most tangelos and tangors. All mandarin varieties are most commonly eaten out-of-hand.

For the cook who enjoys adding the segments whole to salads or sauces, the small, seedless varieties of mandarins are best. Their addition to any dish, even as a garnish, should be well thought out, for they add so much sweetness and flavor that they will dominate a salad, for example, even if only a few segments are tossed in.

Seedless mandarin segments can

be a great foil for grain dishes: in a sauce over buckwheat crêpes, mixed with couscous or bulgur wheat, or with rice and milk, cinnamon, and honey for breakfast. Their sweetness lends itself to sorbets, ice creams, light mousses, and other chilled desserts. The peel of the mandarin and its hybrids can be broken and dried in the oven, then used as flavoring in Chinese stir-fried dishes.

Remember that although varieties differ, the sweetest of the mandarin group are the mandarins themselves. (Take advantage of the juiciness of some varieties and serve glasses of fresh-squeezed mandarin juice garnished with a sprig of mint. It is like nectar.) The tangelos have an overtone of grapefruit flavor (more or less, according to variety), and the tangor resembles the orange in flavor.

All varieties of mandarins, tangelos, and tangors are best when they are heavy and full of juice. Although some varieties are naturally puffy, avoid fruits that are extremely puffy, with very soft spots. Mandarins are usually available in markets from November to May, and more varieties are becoming available for the consumer to enjoy.

Above: 'Orlando' tangelo, a hybrid of 'Duncan' grapefruit and 'Dancy' mandarin.

Right: 'Satsuma' mandarin, one of the hardiest citrus grown commercially.

Orange

Oranges can be sour or sweet. Sweet oranges can be divided into three types: blood oranges, common oranges, and navel oranges.

Blood Orange   Under certain climate conditions, blood oranges develop pink or red flesh, juice, and rind. Many people think their distinctive flavor, usually described as berrylike, is the most delicious of all the oranges.

The development of the red pigmentation is erratic and undependable. It is definitely climate related, but the exact reasons for coloration are not completely understood. The color is intense some years, while in others there is no pigmentation. Even fruit on the same tree will vary in coloration.

Trees grown in the interior valleys of California seem to produce fruit with the most consistent color. Intense color does not develop in fruit grown in cool coastal areas of California or in the humid climates along the Gulf Coast.

Tree size differs among blood orange varieties. 'Sanguinelli' and 'Moro' are smaller and more compact than most other sweet oranges. 'Tarocco' and 'Ruby' are larger and will grow to about the size of other sweet oranges.

Common Orange   Common oranges are divided into two groups: those adapted to the Southwest and those adapted to the Southeast. 'Valencia', the most widely grown variety, is an exception; it is widely planted in both areas and throughout the commercial citrus areas of the world. Common oranges are usually used to make fresh juice. The trees are generally about the same size as navel orange trees.

Navel Orange   Navel oranges are distinguished by the presence of an undeveloped secondary fruit opposite the stem end. As this fruit enlarges, it forms the small hole in the bottom of the fruit known as the "navel."

'Washington' is by far the most widely planted navel orange. The ease with which it peels and separates into segments and its crisp flesh make it the most popular dessert orange.

Navel oranges are genetically unstable. Mutations (sports) occur frequently that may be vegetatively propagated. Most are inferior to the 'Washington' navel, but several have been perpetuated because of their bright color or early bearing habit. 'Atwood', 'Robertson', and 'Skaggs Bonanza' are sports commonly grown in California. 'Dream', 'Glen', and 'Surprise' are sometimes seen in Florida and Texas, where they may perform better than 'Washington'.

All navel oranges are best adapted to intermediate climates of California.

Standard navel oranges reach 16 to 20 feet high; sports are smaller and slower growing.

Sour Orange   Sour oranges are not widely grown for their fruit because their flavor is very bitter. The fruit is used, however, to make orange marmalade and various liqueurs. The trees are often used as ornamentals because of the clean foliage, brightly colored fruit, and fragrant flowers.

The varieties 'Bouquet de Fleurs' and 'Chinotto' are especially useful in the landscape because of their distinctive foliage and compact growth habit.

Sweet Oranges at the Table

Blood Orange   For the cook, the blood orange does not have the versatility of seedless common and navel oranges because of its seeds, nor the piquant flavor of the sour orange. But the bright red color of the fruit—especially the very dark crimson of the 'Moro' variety—makes a lasting impression,

Top Left: *'Bouquet de Fleurs', a sour orange prized for its fragrant blossoms.*

Far Left: *'Ruby' blood orange often develops a red blush on the rind.*

Left: *'Robertson' navel*

particularly when the juice is squeezed and served in a clear juice glass. Cut into wedges or slices, the blood orange can make a dramatic garnish on appropriate fish dishes, atop certain creamed soups, in salads, and on dull dinner plates. Maltaise sauce, a variation on the lemon-flavored Hollandaise sauce, is made with the juice and zest of the blood orange. A tart made with the thickened juice of a dark blood orange, or an ice made with its juice and a bit of zest, will be unforgettable.

Common and Navel Oranges
The essential oil of the orange is used to flavor custards, creams, doughs, stews, soups, pastries, and cookies. Add the flavor of orange flower water and the odor of bergamot, and you will find the scent of sweet orange at every turn.

Whereas the oils of orange zest (the thin, pigmented portion of the rind) can permeate a dish, the flesh of the sweet orange (including the conveniently seedless navel orange) can be a subtle complement or foil for foods with a wide variety of textures and flavors. Remove the pith, seeds, and pips (small, undeveloped seeds) from the sweet orange, slice it thinly, and serve it with Greek or French black olives, thinly sliced raw fennel bulb, purple onion, radishes or daikon, or with watercress or other bitter greens, and a mild vinaigrette: The combinations make a complex salad course. Or serve the slices well chilled and sprinkled with orange-flavored liqueur and finely granulated sugar in a traditional *salade d'orange*. Nothing could be more refreshing.

Serve sweet orange juice as a beverage in itself, chilled, or as an ingredient in a liquid concoction. The seeded sweet orange varieties are particularly sweet and juicy,

Top Right: *This moist orange and almond cake is glazed with orange slices and apricot preserves.*

Bottom Right: *Sweet orange: Citrus sinensis 'Marrs'*

Far Right: *The juice of the blood orange has a striking color and delicious flavor—orange with a hint of raspberry.*

and the seeds can be strained out easily. In the winter, make hot mulled wine with a little orange juice, dry red wine, cinnamon sticks, cloves, sugar, orange and lemon slices, and a drop of angostura bitters; in the summer, serve a pitcher of iced sangria made with sweetened orange juice, a nice burgundy, soda, and orange slices.

The following recipe uses sweet oranges to make a delicious, moist cake that keeps for days.

Sweet Orange and Almond Cake

- 3 small oranges
- 1 lemon
- 1⅔ cups blanched almonds (6 oz)
- 4 eggs
- ½ teaspoon salt
- 1½ cups sugar
- 1 cup flour
- 3 teaspoons baking powder
- ⅔ cup olive oil
- ⅔ cup apricot preserves

1. Place 2 of the oranges and the lemon into 3 inches of water in saucepan, bring to a boil, and simmer for 30 minutes. Drain and let cool. Cut off the stem ends, and cut the fruit in half. Scoop out the pulp and seeds of the lemon and discard; chop the oranges (with rind) and lemon rind very fine, by hand or in a food processor (you will get about 1½ cups). Turn into a sieve and drain, pressing with back of spoon.

2. Preheat oven to 350° F. Chop almonds in a blender until almost as fine as crumbs.

3. In a bowl beat eggs with salt until very thick and light. Gradually beat in sugar.

4. Mix flour and baking powder; stir into the egg mixture until blended. Mix in the fruit, ground almonds, and olive oil.

5. Oil a 9-inch springform pan, and turn batter into prepared pan. Bake until a knife inserted into the center comes out clean, about 1 hour. Allow the cake to cool completely before removing sides of pan.

6. Melt the apricot preserves in a saucepan. Slice the remaining orange into thin slices and simmer 10 minutes in the melted preserves over low heat. Arrange the orange slices decoratively on the cake, and pour the remaining preserves over the cake, making a thin glaze.

Serves 8.

Sour Oranges at the Table

Though well known throughout the Western world, sour oranges are not usually available at the produce market, perhaps because they make for tart juice and sour eating out-of-hand. But for marmalade, no other orange can compare. The sour orange supplies a much more pungent, tart orange flavor than do the sweet oranges. And, like all citrus, the sour orange is rich in pectin (the pith of oranges is one of the sources of commercially produced pectin) and acid. It is therefore easy to make a fine, firm marmalade without adding pectin. (Some store-bought marmalades contain added pectin because the high temperatures used in their cooking methods break down the natural pectins.)

Pummelo

Pummelos are often two to three times larger than grapefruit. They are very popular in the Orient, but have only just recently caught the eye of American gardeners. Varieties are available with white or pink flesh. 'Chandler', a pink variety, is the most widely available. Some Oriental varieties may be available locally in Florida and California.

Most pummelos are large, spreading trees that grow 15 to 18 feet high and equally as wide. The fruit is borne in clusters among the huge, deep green leaves.

Pummelos at the Table

The pummelo can create quite a stir at the table, if only because of its huge dimensions. Although it looks like a very large grapefruit, most pummelo varieties are sweeter and less acidic than grapefruit, with a thicker peel and firmer, less juicy flesh. Its sections are sometimes irregular, creating a mosaic pattern when halved. The pummelo is best eaten peeled and segmented, with the membranes removed.

Because pummelos are not widely grown commercially, they appear in the market after the first of the year for only a few months, despite the fact that they mature at the same time as grapefruit. Choose the heavier (juicier) fruit, with solid yellow skin.

Citrus Relatives

Many citrus relatives are exceptionally handsome plants that are very useful in the landscape. These are some of the best:

Orange jessamine (*Murraya paniculata*) has small, dense, shiny green leaves and makes an excellent hedge. Clusters of powerfully fragrant white flowers are followed by inedible, bright red fruit. This shrub grows 5 to 15 feet high and is hardy to about 25° F.

The foliage of the wampi (*Clausena lansium*) has a coarser texture than most members of the citrus family and grows to about 25 feet high. Its large, white flower clusters are followed by small, edible, yellowish brown fruit.

Although not the most beautiful member of the citrus family, the trifoliate orange (*Poncirus trifoliata*) is a very hardy, deciduous plant that can be grown in cold climates as far north as Washington, D.C. Its growth is very thorny and its fruit is very seedy and acidic, but it makes an effective barrier or hedge. The variety 'Flying Dragon', which shows great promise as a dwarfing rootstock, makes a very pretty bonsai or container plant.

Left: *'Chandler' pummelo*

Above: Poncirus trifoliata—*seedy and sour*

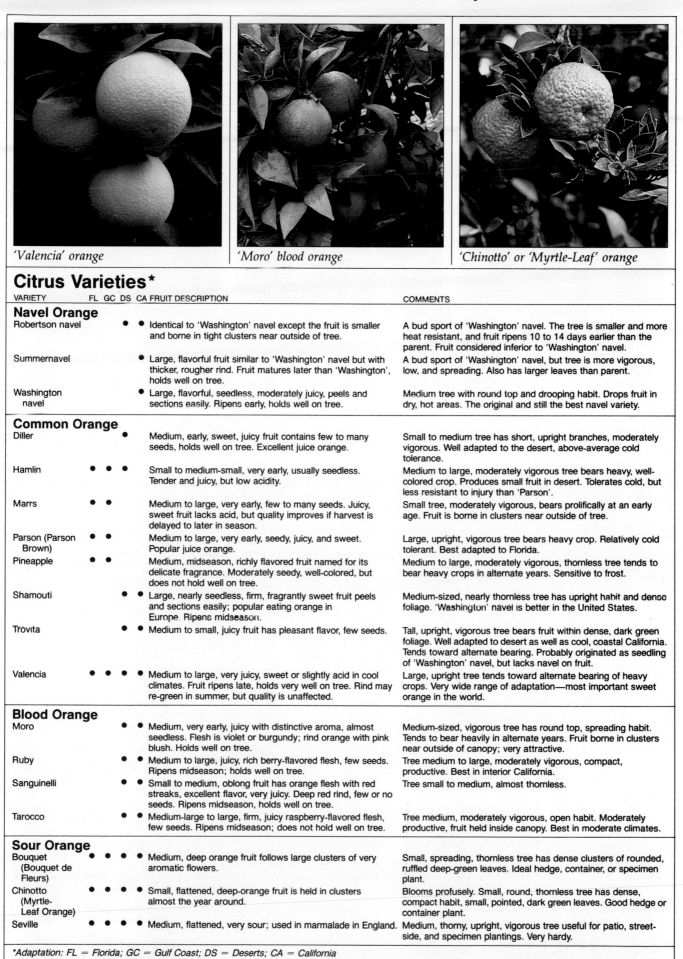

'Valencia' orange   *'Moro' blood orange*   *'Chinotto' or 'Myrtle-Leaf' orange*

Citrus Varieties*

VARIETY	FL	GC	DS	CA	FRUIT DESCRIPTION	COMMENTS
Navel Orange						
Robertson navel	•			•	Identical to 'Washington' navel except the fruit is smaller and borne in tight clusters near outside of tree.	A bud sport of 'Washington' navel. The tree is smaller and more heat resistant, and fruit ripens 10 to 14 days earlier than the parent. Fruit considered inferior to 'Washington' navel.
Summernavel				•	Large, flavorful fruit similar to 'Washington' navel but with thicker, rougher rind. Fruit matures later than 'Washington', holds well on tree.	A bud sport of 'Washington' navel, but tree is more vigorous, low, and spreading. Also has larger leaves than parent.
Washington navel				•	Large, flavorful, seedless, moderately juicy, peels and sections easily. Ripens early, holds well on tree.	Medium tree with round top and drooping habit. Drops fruit in dry, hot areas. The original and still the best navel variety.
Common Orange						
Diller			•		Medium, early, sweet, juicy fruit contains few to many seeds, holds well on tree. Excellent juice orange.	Small to medium tree has short, upright branches, moderately vigorous. Well adapted to the desert, above-average cold tolerance.
Hamlin	•	•	•		Small to medium-small, very early, usually seedless. Tender and juicy, but low acidity.	Medium to large, moderately vigorous tree bears heavy, well-colored crop. Produces small fruit in desert. Tolerates cold, but less resistant to injury than 'Parson'.
Marrs	•	•			Medium to large, very early, few to many seeds. Juicy, sweet fruit lacks acid, but quality improves if harvest is delayed to later in season.	Small tree, moderately vigorous, bears prolifically at an early age. Fruit is borne in clusters near outside of tree.
Parson (Parson Brown)	•	•			Medium to large, very early, seedy, juicy, and sweet. Popular juice orange.	Large, upright, vigorous tree bears heavy crop. Relatively cold tolerant. Best adapted to Florida.
Pineapple	•	•			Medium, midseason, richly flavored fruit named for its delicate fragrance. Moderately seedy, well-colored, but does not hold well on tree.	Medium to large, moderately vigorous, thornless tree tends to bear heavy crops in alternate years. Sensitive to frost.
Shamouti	•			•	Large, nearly seedless, firm, fragrantly sweet fruit peels and sections easily; popular eating orange in Europe. Ripens midseason.	Medium-sized, nearly thornless tree has upright habit and dense foliage. 'Washington' navel is better in the United States.
Trovita	•			•	Medium to small, juicy fruit has pleasant flavor, few seeds.	Tall, upright, vigorous tree bears fruit within dense, dark green foliage. Well adapted to desert as well as cool, coastal California. Tends toward alternate bearing. Probably originated as seedling of 'Washington' navel, but lacks navel on fruit.
Valencia	•	•	•	•	Medium to large, very juicy, sweet or slightly acid in cool climates. Fruit ripens late, holds very well on tree. Rind may re-green in summer, but quality is unaffected.	Large, upright tree tends toward alternate bearing of heavy crops. Very wide range of adaptation—most important sweet orange in the world.
Blood Orange						
Moro	•			•	Medium, very early, juicy with distinctive aroma, almost seedless. Flesh is violet or burgundy; rind orange with pink blush. Holds well on tree.	Medium-sized, vigorous tree has round top, spreading habit. Tends to bear heavily in alternate years. Fruit borne in clusters near outside of canopy; very attractive.
Ruby	•			•	Medium to large, juicy, rich berry-flavored flesh, few seeds. Ripens midseason; holds well on tree.	Tree medium to large, moderately vigorous, compact, productive. Best in interior California.
Sanguinelli	•			•	Small to medium, oblong fruit has orange flesh with red streaks, excellent flavor, very juicy. Deep red rind, few or no seeds. Ripens midseason, holds well on tree.	Tree small to medium, almost thornless.
Tarocco	•			•	Medium-large to large, firm, juicy raspberry-flavored flesh, few seeds. Ripens midseason; does not hold well on tree.	Tree medium, moderately vigorous, open habit. Moderately productive, fruit held inside canopy. Best in moderate climates.
Sour Orange						
Bouquet (Bouquet de Fleurs)	•	•	•	•	Medium, deep orange fruit follows large clusters of very aromatic flowers.	Small, spreading, thornless tree has dense clusters of rounded, ruffled deep-green leaves. Ideal hedge, container, or specimen plant.
Chinotto (Myrtle-Leaf Orange)	•	•	•	•	Small, flattened, deep-orange fruit is held in clusters almost the year around.	Blooms profusely. Small, round, thornless tree has dense, compact habit, small, pointed, dark green leaves. Good hedge or container plant.
Seville	•	•	•	•	Medium, flattened, very sour; used in marmalade in England.	Medium, thorny, upright, vigorous tree useful for patio, street-side, and specimen plantings. Very hardy.

Adaptation: FL = Florida; GC = Gulf Coast; DS = Deserts; CA = California

'Fairchild' mandarin   *'Honey' mandarin*   *'Eureka' lemon*

Citrus Varieties* (continued)

VARIETY	FL	GC	DS	CA	FRUIT DESCRIPTION	COMMENTS
Mandarin Orange						
Calamondin	●	●	●	●	Very small, tender, juicy, acidic, few seeds. Rind sweet and edible. Holds very well on tree.	Small columnar tree has small oval leaves. Very productive and cold-tolerant. Hybrid of mandarin and kumquat.
Changsha		●			Small to medium, early, seedy, with good flavor. Resembles 'Satsuma'.	Very hardy; grown in cold areas of Gulf Coast. Bears early and true to type from seed.
Clementine (Algerian)	●	●	●	●	Medium, early, sweet, juicy, fragrant, red-orange fruit contains few to many seeds, peels easily. Holds well on tree.	Small to medium tree has attractive weeping habit, dense foliage. Needs pollinator such as 'Dancy' or 'Kinnow' mandarin, 'Orlando' tangelo, 'Marrs' or 'Valencia' orange for best fruit production.
Dancy	●	●	●		Medium, midseason, richly flavored, acidic, few to many seeds, does not hold well on tree. Peels and segments easily.	Medium-large, vigorous tree has few thorns. Traditional Christmas tangerine. Best in Florida.
Encore	●	●	●	●	Medium, tender, rich, and juicy. Ripens late season. Colorful, speckled rind peels easily. Holds well on tree.	Medium tree has many upright, spreading branches with few thorns. Tends to bear heavy crops in alternate years. Not widely available, but valuable for late-season fruit.
Honey	●	●	●	●	Small, early, very sweet with many seeds, yellow-orange peel. Holds well on tree.	Tree medium to large, vigorous, spreading. Strong tendency for alternate bearing. Not widely available.
Fairchild	●	●	●		Medium, very early, sweet and juicy, many seeds. Holds fairly well on tree.	Medium, rounded, nearly thornless tree grows vigorously. Best in low deserts of California and Arizona; requires heat.
Kara				●	Medium-large, flavorful fruit remains tart until very mature. Ripens late season; holds fairly well on tree but becomes puffy.	Medium to large, thornless, moderately vigorous tree has drooping habit, large, dark green leaves. Best adapted to interior California. Tendency toward alternate bearing.
Kinnow			●	●	Medium, juicy, richly flavored fruit ripens midseason, holds well on tree.	Large, frost-tolerant, vigorous, columnar tree has many long, slender, thornless branchlets. Attractive ornamental, but strong tendency for alternate bearing.
Mediterranean (Willowleaf)	●	●	●	●	Small to medium, juicy, sweet, aromatic, fruit that deteriorates quickly when mature. Fruit held toward inside of tree.	Small to medium, spreading tree has attractive small, narrow leaves, few thorns. Hardy, but needs high heat for best fruit.
Page	●	●	●	●	Small to medium, early, rich, sweet, with few to many seeds. Holds well on tree. Excellent for juice.	Medium to large, very attractive tree has dense foliage, round top. Almost thornless. Resembles a sweet orange, but technically a mandarin. Not widely available.
Satsuma	●	●		●	Medium, early, mild and sweet with low acid. Holds poorly on tree, but stores well.	Small to medium, slow-growing, spreading tree has open, dark green foliage. Tough and very cold hardy. Popular in Northern California and Gulf Coast. 'Kimbrough' is a new, hardy 'Satsuma'-type mandarin for the Gulf Coast.
Wilking	●	●	●	●	Small to medium, rich and sprightly, very juicy. Holds well on tree with some puffiness.	Small to medium tree has dense, willowlike foliage, few thorns. Cold tolerant and attractive. Strong tendency for alternate bearing; fruit set varies from almost nothing to limb-breaking loads. Not widely available.
Lemon						
Eureka			●	●	Medium, highly acidic, juicy, few seeds. Produces fruit all year along coast, spring and summer inland. Common commercial variety. Best picked when ripe.	Medium, nearly thornless, moderately vigorous tree, open and spreading. Short-lived and sensitive to cold, insects, and neglect.
Improved Meyer	●	●	●	●	Medium, juicy, slightly sweet when mature, excellent flavor. Holds well on tree.	Small to medium, nearly thornless, moderately vigorous tree. Spreading habit, good for hedges and containers. Hardy, productive, and nearly everblooming.
Lisbon			●	●	Medium, highly acidic, juicy, few seeds. Best picked when ripe; loses acidity if left on tree.	Large, vigorous, thorny, upright tree has dense foliage. Flowers and new growth tinged with purple. Most productive and cold hardy of true lemons.
Ponderosa	●		●	●	Grapefruit-sized, juicy, and acidic with thick, fleshy rind. Holds well on tree.	Small, roundheaded, thorny tree has large leaves, blooms all year. Hybrid of lemon and citron; sensitive to frost. Good subject for containers and hedges.

Adaptation: FL = Florida; GC = Gulf Coast; DS = Deserts; CA = California

'Meiwa' kumquat   'Temple' tangor   'Etrog' citron

Citrus Varieties* (continued)

VARIETY	FL	GC	DS	CA	FRUIT DESCRIPTION	COMMENTS
Lime						
Bearss (Tahiti, Persian)	●	●	●	●	Medium-small, acidic, and very juicy. Usually picked green; yellow when mature. Does not hold well on tree.	Medium, vigorous, spreading tree bears fragrant blossoms and shiny fruit all year in cool, coastal areas. Few thorns, hardier and more attractive than 'Mexican'.
Mexican (Key)	●	●	●	●	Very small, juicy, and acidic with distinctive aroma; the "bartender's lime." Commercially picked when green; turns yellow and drops from tree when mature.	Medium, twiggy tree has dense canopy of small leaves, many short thorns. Moderately vigorous. Very frost sensitive, needs long, hot summers.
Rangpur	●	●	●	●	Small to medium, very acidic and juicy. Rind is reddish-orange when mature; fruit holds very well on tree.	Medium, vigorous tree has spreading, drooping habit, few thorns. Very cold-tolerant. Not a true lime (resembles mandarin) but often used as a lime substitute. 'Otaheite' is an acidless, semidwarf form popular for containers.
Grapefruit						
Duncan	●	●			Large, somewhat early, seedy, very juicy, white flesh. Excellent flavor. Holds well on tree.	Large, vigorous, productive tree. Attractive habit, dark green foliage. Reputed to be most cold-tolerant grapefruit.
Marsh	●	●	●	●	Medium, late maturing, seedless, very juicy. Holds extremely well on tree, stores well.	Large, vigorous, spreading tree requires high summer heat. Attractive clusters of fruit, glossy leaves.
Oroblanco			●	●	Medium to large, early, seedless, extremely juicy, white flesh. Distinctive, sweet flavor. Does not hold well on tree.	Large tree. Recently introduced pummelo-grapefruit hybrid. Best in interior California.
Redblush (Ruby, Red Marsh)	●	●	●	●	Medium, midseason, similar to 'Marsh' except flesh and rind have crimson tinge. Holds very well on tree.	Large, vigorous tree identical to 'Marsh'.
Star Ruby	●		●	●	Medium, midseason, seedless, juicy, deep red flesh. Fruit holds well on tree.	Medium tree. Developed for Texas; needs heat.
Kumquat						
Nagami	●	●	●	●	Small, oval, rind is slightly sweet, flesh acidic, little juice. Used primarily for canning. Holds very well on tree.	Small to medium, vigorous tree has small, dark green leaves, fine branches. Excellent container plant. Very cold tolerant.
Meiwa	●	●	●	●	Small, round fruit sweeter, juicier, and larger than 'Nagami'; good for fresh eating. Holds very well on tree.	Small to medium tree with smaller leaves and more open habit than 'Nagami'. Very cold tolerant.
Limequat						
Eustis	●	●	●	●	Medium, sweet, and juicy, light yellow when mature; resembles lime when immature.	Hybrid of Mexican lime and kumquat; tree resembles lime but is much more cold tolerant. Attractive, nearly thornless, suitable for containers. 'Lakeland' is very similar variety.
Orangequat						
Nippon	●	●	●	●	Medium, sweet, and juicy, rind and pulp deep orange. Larger than the kumquats.	Small, attractive, compact tree.
Pummelo						
Chandler	●	●	●	●	Very large, flesh is pink and tender, moderately juicy. Sweet, aromatic flavor. Rind yellow, thick, and smooth.	Large, open, vigorous tree has large leaves, large woody flowers. Needs hot summers for best production.
Tangelo						
Minneola	●	●	●	●	Large, richly-flavored and tart. Rind reddish orange; flesh orange, few seeds. Ripens late midseason.	Medium to large, vigorous, attractive tree has large, pointed leaves, rounded habit. For best production cross-pollinate with 'Dancy', 'Clementine', or 'Kinnow' mandarins, or 'Valencia' orange. Not compatible with 'Orlando' tangelo.
Orlando	●	●	●	●	Medium-large, very early, juicy, and mildly sweet. Orange rind and flesh. Does not hold well on tree.	Leaves are distinctly cupped. Less vigorous and more cold tolerant than 'Minneola'. Needs pollinator such as 'Dancy', 'Clementine', or 'Kinnow' mandarins, or 'Temple' tangor. Not compatible with 'Minneola' tangelo.
Tangor						
Temple	●		●		Medium-large, seedy, rich and spicy. Ripens mid- to late season; holds fairly well on tree.	Small to medium, moderately vigorous, spreading, bushy tree. More sensitive to cold than mandarins and oranges.
Murcott (Murcott Honey)	●				Medium, rich and juicy, few to many seeds. Thin, yellow-orange rind does not peel easily. Ripens mid- to late season. Does not hold well on tree.	Tree is medium in size and vigor, upright, very cold-sensitive. Also classified as mandarin, and sometimes sold as 'Honey', but origin unknown.

*Adaptation: FL = Florida; GC = Gulf Coast; DS = Deserts; CA = California

Feijoa

The feijoa is an attractive shrub that bears delicious fruit with an unusual and refreshing pineapple-mint flavor. The fruit vary in shape from round to an elongated pear shape. The waxy skin is dull blue-green when harvested but takes on a shiny green appearance if rubbed. The fruit is best when fresh; most people simply cut the fruit in half and scoop out the sweet flesh with a spoon. The seeds are very small and edible, and the flower petals are a refreshing addition to spring salads.

The feijoa doubles handsomely as a landscape shrub. The leaves are soft green on top and silvery un-derneath, flashing nicely in a gentle breeze. In late spring the shrub is covered with inch-wide white flowers with scarlet stamens. Feijoa responds very well to pruning or shearing, but wait until early summer—after you've enjoyed the flowers. When planted close together, the shrubs make a nice hedge, screen, or windbreak. Feijoa can also be espaliered or trained as a small tree (20 to 25 feet tall) with one or more trunks.

Adaptation

Feijoas are widely adapted to areas of the West and Southeast where winter temperatures do not fall below 15° F. The highest-quality fruit is produced in areas with moderate summers (80° to 90° F) and cool winters. A small amount of winter chilling (between 100 and 200 hours) ensures an abundant bloom. Fruit production is unreliable in southernmost Florida, where fewer than 50 hours of chilling occur.

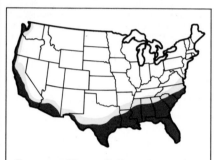

Common Name: Feijoa, pineapple guava.

Botanical Name: *Feijoa sellowiana*.

Origin: Southern Brazil, Paraguay, Uruguay, northern Argentina.

Growth Habit: Slow-growing evergreen shrub that can reach 15 feet high and 15 feet wide.

Adaptation: Prefers cool winters and moderate summers, but generally adapted to areas where temperatures stay above 15° F. Poor flower production in areas with fewer than 50 hours of chilling.

Harvest Season: September through November in North America. Fruit from New Zealand is available in supermarkets in midspring.

Begins Bearing: Grafted or cutting-grown plants require 2 to 3 years. Seedlings, which have unpredictable quality, take 4 to 6 years.

Propagation: Cuttings, layering, and grafting. Unreliable by seed.

Maintenance: Low.

Pollination: Some self-sterility; plant 2 different varieties for maximum yields.

Suitability for Containers: Ideal container plant.

Landscape Quality: Excellent. Makes a beautiful hedge.

Nurseries: E, I, O, P, S, U, Y.

Information: 1, 2, 8, 13, 14.

Top: *In addition to being very showy, the blossoms of* Feijoa sellowiana *have edible petals—a delightful addition to spring salads.* Bottom: *Feijoas are always attractive. The silvery shades of the leaf undersides contrast with the deeper green of the upper leaf surfaces.*

Even though the plants are relatively hardy, sudden fall frosts can damage ripening fruit and late spring frosts can destroy blossoms. Spring frost damage is most likely in mild-winter areas, where the plants are not completely hardened off and respond to warm spells by blooming early. In colder areas the plants don't usually flower until after the danger of frost has passed.

Propagation

The seeds of the feijoa germinate easily, but the seedlings grow slowly and rarely produce quality fruit. Success with cuttings, even under mist, differs among varieties. Various grafting methods are sometimes successful, as is layering.

Because the plants sucker readily, grafted plants must be trained to grow with no branches below the graft union. Cutting-grown plants of named varieties are most desirable, because they can be trained in a variety of ways. Cuttings can be maintained as multitrunked shrubs without concern that suckers will develop into "rogue" branches.

Site Selection and Planting

Feijoa fruit quality declines if the temperature regularly exceeds 100° F, and the fruit can sunburn. Also, when the ripe fruits fall to the ground (a sign of peak quality), they will spoil rapidly at high temperatures. To protect the fruit, choose a planting site away from hot, reflected sun. In desert areas, plant feijoas where they will receive partial shade during the hottest part of the day.

Feijoas will grow in a wide variety of soils. The best harvests, however, come from plants growing in well-drained soil with a pH between 5.5 and 7.0. The plants are fairly salt tolerant, but salinity slows growth and reduces yields.

Caring for Feijoas

Watering   The thick leaves of feijoa do not show signs of moisture stress as quickly as do those of most other plants. They can survive considerable drought, but lack of water will cause the fruit to drop. For quality harvests, water deeply on a regular basis and mulch the soil around the plants to protect the shallow roots.

Fertilizing   Feijoa plants grow slowly and require only light applications of a complete fertilizer, if anything at all.

Pruning   Cutting-grown plants can be developed as shrubs with single or multiple trunks. Grafted plants must have a single trunk below graft union. See "Propagation," above.

Pruning is not required to keep plants productive, but a light pruning in the summer after the fruit is harvested will encourage new growth and increase yields the following year. You may want to thin the plant for easier harvesting. When grown as a hedge, the feijoa responds well to heavy pruning or shearing, but this reduces flower and fruit production.

Pests and Diseases   Feijoas rarely have any serious problems.

Harvest and Storage

As the fruit matures, its color changes almost imperceptibly. The best way to tell when the fruit are fully ripe is to allow them to fall from the tree. Giving the tree a shake and gathering feijoas from the ground every couple of days is the usual method of harvesting. To keep the fruit from bruising, place a tarp or other large cloth under the tree to catch them as they fall. This will also help keep the fruit clean and free of the soil organisms that promote spoilage. Feijoas can also be picked when firm and mature and allowed to ripen at room temperature.

Mature fruit can be stored in the refrigerator for about a week, but after that the quality declines rapidly.

Feijoas at the Table

The feijoa is high in acid and pectin and makes excellent jellies and preserves. Fresh feijoas can be quartered and eaten out-of-hand, or sliced and used as a garnish. Sliced feijoas also add a new dimension to fresh fruit compote. The edible white flower petals enhance salads and ice cream or provide a lovely garnish for plain dishes. If you pluck the petals carefully, the flowers will still develop into fruit.

Feijoa Varieties

VARIETY	FRUIT DESCRIPTION	COMMENTS
Apollo	Large, oblong, excellent quality but slightly gritty. Ripens early.	Self-fertile, upright, spreading plant. Productive.
Choiceana	Small to medium, oblong, fair to good quality. Ripens midseason.	Self-sterile, must be cross-pollinated.
Coolidge	Small to medium, pear-shaped, fair to good quality. Ripens late.	Productive. Self-fertile. Variable fruit size.
Edenvale Improved Coolidge	Large, oblong, quality very good to excellent. Ripens late.	Productive. Self-fertile. Grows slowly.
Edenvale Late	Medium, oblong, quality very good to excellent. Ripens late.	Very productive. Self-fertile. Grows slowly.
Edenvale Supreme	Medium, oblong, quality very good to excellent. Ripens late.	Productive. Self-fertile. Grows slowly. Best eaten soon after harvest.
Gemini	Medium, pear-shaped, very good quality. Ripens late.	Productive. Best fruit quality if cross-pollinated. Upright, spreading tree.
Magnifica	Large, oblong, fair quality. Ripens midseason.	Bears few fruit. Self-fertile.
Mammoth	Small to large, good quality. Thick skin, gritty flesh. Ripens midseason.	Self-fertile but bears larger fruit with cross-pollination. Vigorous plant.
Nazemetz	Large, pear-shaped fruit, thin skin, sweet pulp; excellent quality. Ripens late.	Self-fertile. One of the best varieties.
Pineapple Gem	Small, round, very good quality. Ripens late.	Poor in cool, coastal conditions. Bears heavier yields if cross-pollinated.
Superba	Small, round, fair to good quality. Ripens late.	Self-sterile; must be cross-pollinated.
Trask	Medium, round, fair to good quality. Thick skin, gritty flesh. Ripens midseason.	Self-sterile; must be cross-pollinated. Vigorous plant.
Triumph	Small, pear-shaped, good to very good quality. Thick skin, gritty flesh. Ripens midseason.	Bears heavier yields if cross-pollinated. Vigorous plant.

Fig

Fig trees have a dramatic presence wherever they are grown. Their silvery gray branches are muscular and twisting, spreading wider than they are tall. The leaves are unusually large (4 to 10 inches long) and bright green, with three to five rounded lobes. In winter the trees provide a strong silhouette against cloudy skies; in summer, their foliage lends a beautiful tropical feeling.

Besides high marks for beauty, figs are relatively easy to grow and are remarkably adaptable. They are productive with or without heavy pruning. Even if the plant is frozen to the ground in the winter, it can often spring back and bear fruit the following summer. In containers, figs are eye-catching specimens, indoors or outdoors.

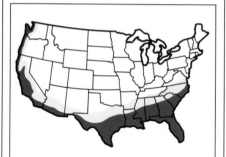

Common Name: Fig.

Botanical Name: *Ficus carica.*

Origin: Eastern Mediterranean and southwestern Asia.

Growth Habit: Deciduous tree. Can reach 60 feet but usually grows 15 to 30 feet high. Wide-spreading. Can be maintained at almost any size with pruning.

Adaptation: Hardy to 12° to 15° F if fully dormant. Best fruit quality in hot, dry climates. Chilling requirement less than 300 hours.

Harvest Season: Often two crops, one in late spring, another in fall.

Begins Bearing: Early, often first year after planting.

Propagation: Hardwood or softwood cuttings, air-layering, and root suckers.

Maintenance: Low.

Pollination: Common varieties are self-fruitful.

Suitability for Containers: Well suited.

Landscape Quality: Excellent.

Nurseries: A, B, D, E, F, G, H, I, J, K, L, N, O, P, Q, R, S, V.

Information: 1, 3, 8, 9, 10, 14.

Although the fig is commonly called a fruit, it is really a cluster of outside-in, fleshy flowers. Each flower can develop into a seed if pollinated. The fruit may seem to contain slightly crunchy seeds, but these are actually undeveloped seedless fruitlets that are not viable.

There are basically four types of fig: the common fig, Caprifig, Smyrna fig, and San Pedro fig. Only varieties of the common fig will set two crops of fruit without pollination. The first crop is borne in spring on the last season's growth and is called the breba crop. The second crop is borne in the fall on the new growth and is known as the main crop. In cold climates the breba crop is often destroyed by spring frosts. It is also limited by pruning.

Caprifigs and Smyrna figs are rarely offered to home gardeners, because pollination from a specific type of wasp is necessary for fruit production. These wasps are usually not found in North America. San Pedro figs produce a breba crop

without pollination, and will grow in cool summer climates.

Adaptation

Figs are generally best adapted to areas with long, hot summers. Most commercial fig plantations are found in the warm interior valleys of California. Some fig varieties, however, require less heat to ripen their fruit and can be grown in cooler climates with short summers. In such areas figs are usually seen as shrubs, having frozen to the ground in the winter. Mulching and wise site selection are very important to successful fig culture in colder climates.

When fully dormant, a fig tree can withstand temperatures of 12° to 15° F. In the late spring and early fall the trees are more sensitive and can be damaged at higher temperatures. Because of their low chilling requirements, figs will sometimes break dormancy during warm spells in the winter or early spring, only to be damaged when cold weather returns.

Figs adapt well to hot, dry, desert climates and will survive periods of drought, although fruit quality is much better with regular irrigation.

In the Southeast, where the dried fruit beetle is a serious pest, gardeners are limited to growing varieties that have fruit with a closed eye. The eye is the small hole in the plump end of a fig through which the flowers are pollinated when grown in its native habitat. If the dried fruit beetle enters the eye, the fruit is usually ruined.

Top: *Its strong, spreading branches and large, deciduous leaves make the fig an ideal specimen or shade tree.* Bottom: *'Magnolia' figs are at their best when eaten fresh.*

Propagation

Figs are easily propagated from dormant hardwood cuttings. Select one-year-old, fully mature shoots, ⅜ to ⅝ inch in diameter and 8 to 12 inches long. Bury them upright in the soil, leaving one node exposed. If freezing weather is expected, cover the whips completely or bring them indoors for protection. By spring the ends of the cuttings should have a soft white callus growth. Transplanted or left in place, the new plants should be well rooted and established by the end of the summer.

Site Selection and Planting

Choose a planting site with full sun and well-drained soil. Figs will tolerate a variety of soils as long as they are not very salty or alkaline. In areas with short (less than 120 days between frosts), cool summers, espalier trees against a south-facing, light-colored wall to take advantage of the reflected heat.

Caring for Fig Trees

Established fig trees can survive with a minimum of watering, fertilizing, and pruning. For a top-quality harvest, however, you should probably do a little of each.

Watering Young fig trees should be watered regularly until fully established. In dry western climates, water mature trees deeply at least every one or two weeks. Desert gardeners may have to water more frequently. Southern gardeners may need to water only in dry spells. Mulch the soil around the trees to conserve moisture. If a tree is not getting enough water, the leaves will turn yellow and drop. Also, drought-stressed trees are more susceptible to nematode damage.

Fertilizing Fertilizer recommendations vary depending on where you live. Just make sure you don't overdo it. Too much nitrogen causes excess foliage growth at the expense of fruit production, and the fruit that is produced often ripens improperly, if at all.

As a general rule, fertilize fig trees if the branches grew less than a foot during the previous year. Apply a total of ½ to 1 pound of actual nitrogen, divided into three or four applications beginning in

Fig Varieties

VARIETY	FRUIT DESCRIPTION*	COMMENTS
Adriatic (Verdone, White Adriatic, Strawberry Fig)	Small to medium, skin is greenish, flesh strawberry colored. Good, all-purpose fig.	Light breba crop. Large, vigorous tree leafs out early; subject to frost damage. Prune to force new growth.
Alma	Medium, skin is light yellow, flesh amber-tan. Very sweet. Good fresh or dried.	Light breba crop, heavy main crop. Requires long, warm summers; well adapted to the Southeast, small eye. Hardy, small tree.
Beall	Large, skin is dark purple, flesh dark purplish red. Very sweet.	Large breba crop. Similar to 'Brown Turkey'.
Black Mission (Mission, Franciscan, California Large Black)	Large, skin is purplish black, flesh pink. Excellent, all-purpose fig.	Good breba crop of large fruit. Large, vigorous tree produces best when not heavily pruned. Main California commercial variety.
Blanche (White Marseille, Lattarula, Italian Honey Fig, Lemon)	Medium to large, skin is yellowish green, flesh white to amber. Very sweet, lemon flavor.	Light breba crop. Valuable in short-season, cool-summer areas. Slow-growing, dense, hardy tree.
Brown Turkey (San Piero, San Piero Black, California Large Black)	Medium, skin is purplish brown, flesh pinkish amber. Good flavor; best when fresh.	Light breba crop. Small, hardy, vigorous tree. Prune severely for heaviest main crop.
Celeste (Blue Celeste, Celestial, Honey Fig, Malta, Sugar, Violette)	Small to medium, skin is light violet to violet-brown, flesh reddish amber. Very sweet, usually dried.	Light breba crop. Tightly closed eye; good for Southeast. Small, productive, hardy.
Conadria	Medium, skin is greenish yellow to white with purplish blush, flesh strawberry. Mildly sweet. Good fresh, excellent dried.	Early breba crop. Vigorous tree, best in hot climates.
Everbearing (Texas Everbearing, Eastern Brown Turkey)	Medium to large, skin is thick and mahogany-purple, flesh strawberry, best fresh.	Light breba crop. Best adapted to cool areas of the South. Vigorous but spreading. Prune to force new growth.
Excell	Large, skin is yellow, flesh light amber. Very sweet. Excellent, all-purpose fig.	Light breba crop. Similar to 'Kadota' but more productive. Fruit has small eye; good for Southeast. Vigorous tree.
Flanders	Medium, long neck, skin is brownish yellow with violet stripes, flesh amber. Strong, fine flavor. Excellent, all-purpose fruit.	Good breba crop. Ripens late.
Genoa (White Genoa)	Medium, skin is greenish yellow to white, flesh yellow-amber. Sweet, good fresh or dried.	Light breba and main crops. Fruit has large eye and hollow center. Best adapted to cooler regions of the West.
Kadota (White Kadota, Dottato, Florentine)	Medium, skin is yellowish green, flesh amber. Rich flavor, excellent, all-purpose fig.	Little or no breba crop. Requires hot, dry climate for best quality. Vigorous tree.
King (Desert King)	Large, skin is dark green, flesh purple. Sweet, delicious fresh or dried.	Good breba crop; no main crop. Hardy, best adapted to cool areas such as the Pacific Northwest. Do not prune severely.
Magnolia (Madonna, Brunswick)	Medium, skin is reddish brown, flesh strawberry. Does not dry well.	Light breba crop. Develops best flavor and size with caprification. Vigorous, hardy tree.
Osborne Prolific (Neveralla, Archipel)	Medium to large, skin is dark reddish brown, flesh amber. Very sweet, best fresh.	Light breba crop. Hardy. Best in areas with cool, short summers, such as coastal California. Poor in warm climates.
Panachee (Tiger Fig, Striped Tiger)	Small to medium, skin is greenish yellow with dark green stripes, flesh strawberry, dry but sweet. Best fresh.	No breba crop. Unusual-looking fig; requires long, warm growing season. Ripens late. Medium eye.
Pasquale (Verino)	Small, skin is dark purplish black, flesh dark strawberry. Fine flavor, very sweet. Excellent fresh or dried.	Good breba crop. Main crop ripens very late; susceptible to fall frost damage.
Tena	Small, skin is light green, flesh amber. Fine flavor. Good fresh or dried.	Good breba crop. Bears heavily. Medium eye.
Venture	Large, skin is green, flesh deep red, long neck. Excellent flavor, good fresh or dried.	Good breba crop. Ripens late but matures well in cool areas. Compact tree.
Verte (Green Ischia)	Small, skin is greenish yellow, flesh strawberry. Excellent fresh or dried.	Good breba crop. Small tree. Recommended for short-summer climates.

Ripening periods vary by area. Breba crops usually ripen between late June and late August. Main crops ripen from late August to the first frost.

Growing Figs in Cold Climates

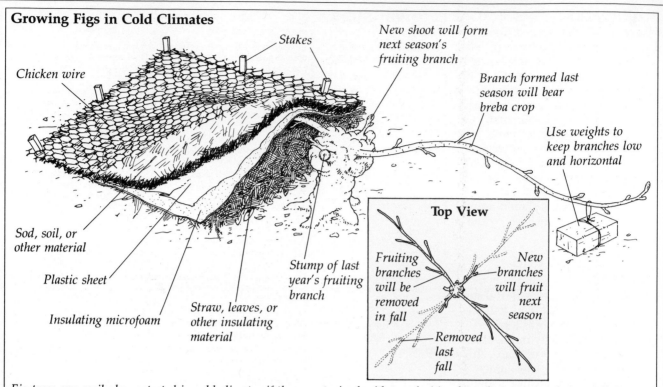

Fig trees can easily be protected in cold climates if they are trained with two fruiting branches growing from one low trunk. During the growing season, select shoots growing from the trunk at a 90-degree angle to the limbs currently bearing fruit. These will bear next year's breba crop. Remove the branches that bore fruit in the fall before covering the plant.

late winter or early spring and ending in July. Use the same time-tables for younger trees, but use a balanced fertilizer according to the instructions on the fertilizer label.

Pruning   Young figs should be pruned to establish a strong frame-work. After that, prune occasional-ly to remove deadwood and to keep the trees from becoming over-grown. Thin occasionally to keep the inner branches productive.

Even though they can get along without it, mature fig trees respond very well to pruning. They can be espaliered or pruned heavily for size control without sacrificing the main crop if pruned when dor-mant. In fact, dormant-season pruning can increase the main crop. Dormant-season pruning re-moves flower buds and thus re-duces or eliminates the breba crop.

Pests and Diseases   Aside from fruit flies, which infest fruit with open eyes grown in the Southeast, fig trees are susceptible to very few diseases or pests.

Harvest and Storage

Figs must be allowed to ripen fully on the tree before they are picked. They will not ripen if picked when immature. A ripe fruit will be slightly soft and starting to bend at the neck. Harvest the fruit gently to avoid bruising them.

Some people are sensitive to the foliage and milky white sap of the fig tree. If you have sensitive skin, wear a long-sleeved shirt and gloves while harvesting.

Fresh figs do not keep well; they can be stored in the refrigerator for only two to three days.

Some fig varieties are delicious when dried. In hot, dry climates, figs that are to be dried should be collected as they drop from the tree. In humid or wet climates, the fruit should be picked as ripe as possible but before they fall. Before drying, peel and quarter the fruit. Figs take 4 to 5 days to dry in the sun, 10 to 12 hours in a dehydrator. When dry, the fruit should be pli-able and slightly sticky, but not wet. Dried figs can be stored for six to eight months.

Figs at the Table

Fig lovers usually prefer fresh figs. Serve them peeled and quartered on a bed of dressed bitter greens such as rocket (this is particularly attractive with the 'Mission' fig), wrapped in prosciutto and secured with a toothpick, or accompanied by Gorgonzola cheese for dessert.

The pickled figs in the following recipe are a good accompaniment for game, ham, or lamb, and make a delicious (and quick) dessert topped with whipped cream cheese or crème fraîche.

Spiced Figs

- 6 pounds ripe figs, stems trimmed
- 1 cup water
- 1 cup distilled white vinegar
- 4 cups sugar
- ½ teaspoon freshly grated nutmeg
- 8 whole cloves
- 4 bay leaves, broken in two
- 8 slices fresh ginger

1. In a 6- to 8-quart stainless steel or enameled pan, bring the figs, wa-ter, vinegar, sugar, nutmeg, cloves, bay leaves, and ginger to a boil.

2. Reduce heat and simmer, uncov-ered, for 15 minutes.

3. Pour into storage containers and refrigerate, or process according to jar manufacturer's instructions. Dis-tribute the cloves, bay leaf halves, and sliced ginger among the jars.

Makes 7 to 8 pints.

Guava

There are two types of guavas: the tropical guava (*Psidium guajava*) and the strawberry or Cattley guava (*Psidium cattleianum*). The strawberry guava comes in two varieties. One is a red-fruited form, *Psidium cattleianum longipes*, and the other is a yellow-fruited form, *Psidium cattleianum lucidum*, more commonly referred to as the lemon guava. Both types of guava are attractive evergreen plants with shedding bark and fragrant flowers, but they differ in size, fruit quality, and adaptation.

The tropical guava bears egg-shaped fruit ranging in size from 2 to 4 inches long. Tropical guava varieties differ quite a bit in flavor and seediness, but most have a musky aroma. The sweeter varieties with soft seeds are excellent eaten fresh, and all make delicious jams, jellies, preserves and juices. Tropical guavas are borne on large, attractive shrubs or small trees that can reach 20 to 25 feet high. Although usually evergreen, the deeply veined leaves may drop for a brief period in spring.

Strawberry guavas are borne on smaller, extremely handsome plants rarely exceeding 10 to 15 feet high. Because of their beauty, they are often used as ornamentals. The glossy, deep green leaves form a perfect backdrop for the brightly colored fruit, which is preceded, and often accompanied, by sweetly fragrant white flowers. The fruit are smaller than those of the tropical guava, generally an inch or two in diameter. Unfortunately, there are no selected varieties and seedlings vary in quality, but the yellow types are usually larger and sweeter. It's best to propagate plants that you know will produce sweet fruit.

Adaptation

The tropical guava is best adapted to the warm, humid climates of Florida and Hawaii, although it can be grown in coastal Southern California. As its name suggests, the tropical guava is sensitive to frost; a tree will recover from brief exposure to 29° F but may be completely defoliated. The strawberry guava is a much hardier plant, able to withstand brief periods of tempera-

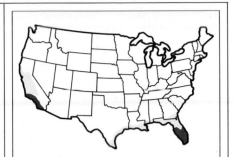

Common Name: Guava.
Botanical Name: *Psidium* species.
Origin: Columbia, Peru, and Brazil.
Growth Habit: Evergreen shrubs to small trees reaching from 10 to 25 feet high.
Adaptation: Varies; see text.
Harvest Season: Fruit ripen over a long period from spring to fall; some ripen the year around.
Begins Bearing: In 2 to 3 years.
Propagation: Air-layering is most reliable, but can also be grown from cuttings or suckers. Seedlings may not produce quality fruit.
Maintenance: Low.
Pollination: Generally self-fruitful, but yields are greater if cross-pollinated.
Suitability for Containers: Excellent indoors or out.
Landscape Quality: Extremely attractive plants. Useful as hedges, screens, or specimens.
Nurseries: A, E, I, O, P, S, U, Y.
Information: 1, 2, 8, 13, 14.

Top: *The fruit of the strawberry guava turns bright red when ripe.* Bottom: Psidium guajava. *For best flavor, guavas should be allowed to ripen on the plant.*

These flowers of the Cattley guava have a sweet fragrance and are self-pollinating.

tures as low as 24° F. Plants are adapted to California but do poorly in hot desert or interior areas.

Pollination

Guavas are primarily self-fruitful, although some strains seem to produce more fruit when cross-pollinated with another variety. Guavas can bloom throughout the year in mild-winter areas, but the heaviest bloom occurs with the onset of warm weather in the spring. The exact time can vary from year to year depending on weather. Because flowers are produced on the current season's growth, pruning can stimulate flowering.

Site Selection and Planting

Both types of guava prefer full sun and well-drained soil in the pH range of 5 to 7. They will tolerate a variety of soils, but produce better in rich soils high in organic matter. The tropical guava will not tolerate salty soils.

Caring for Guavas

In areas where they are well adapted, guavas are one of the easiest tropical plants to grow.

Watering   Guavas are most productive with regular, deep watering, especially the tropical guava. Lack of moisture will delay bloom and cause the fruit to drop. The strawberry guava can withstand brief periods of drought.

Fertilizing   Tropical guavas are fast growers and heavy feeders, and benefit from regular applications of fertilizer. Mature trees may require as much as ½ pound actual nitrogen per year. Apply fertilizer monthly, just prior to heavy pruning. Strawberry guavas are less vigorous and get by with about half as much nitrogen.

Both types of guava may require chelated micronutrient foliar sprays when grown in containers or areas with alkaline or micronutrient-deficient soils.

Pruning   Guavas respond well to pruning and can be used as informal hedges or screens.

Pests and Diseases   Foliage diseases, such as anthracnose, can be a problem in humid climates. They can be controlled with regular fungicide applications. Where present, root-rot nematodes will reduce

plant vigor. Guava whitefly, guava moth, and Caribbean fruit fly can be major problems in southern Florida, but have not been reported in California. Contact your cooperative extension agent for control measures.

Harvest and Storage

In warmer regions guavas will ripen all year. There is a distinctive change in the color and aroma of a guava that has ripened. For the best flavor, allow fruit to ripen on the plant. Guavas can also be picked green-mature and allowed to ripen off the tree at room temperature. Placing the fruit in a brown paper bag with a banana or apple will hasten ripening.

Mature green fruit can be stored for two to five weeks at temperatures between 46° and 50° F and relative humidity of 85 to 95 percent. Fruit that has changed color cannot be stored for extended periods. It bruises easily and will quickly deteriorate or rot.

Guavas at the Table

True guavas have an exceptionally high vitamin content. They are rich in pectin, and are commonly used in jellies and preserves. Guavas can also be eaten out-of-hand, juiced, or combined with other fruits such as bananas and pineapples.

Guava Jelly

5½ cups fresh or canned guava juice

¼ cup lemon juice

1 box (1¾ oz) powdered fruit pectin

7 cups sugar

Measure the juices into a large, deep pot and add pectin. Bring to a boil. Add sugar and bring to a rolling boil for 1½ minutes. Remove from heat and skim off foam. Pour into hot, sterilized jars, leaving ½-inch headspace. Put lids on jars and place them in a boiling water bath for 15 minutes.

Makes 8 cups.

Tropical Guava Varieties

VARIETY	FRUIT DESCRIPTION	COMMENTS
Dessert Varieties		
Detwiler	Medium to large, yellow flesh. Sweet, pleasant flavor.	Originated in California.
Hawaiian Pear	Small, flesh is thick and yellow-white, small seed cavity. Pear flavor.	Originated in Hawaii.
Hong Kong Pink	Medium to large, flesh is thick and pink, few seeds. Sweet, pleasant flavor.	Originated in Hawaii.
Indonesian Seedless	Small to medium, flesh is hard and white, usually seedless. Good flavor.	Originated in Florida.
Lucknow 49	Medium to large, flesh is thick and white, moderately seedy. Sweet, slightly musky.	Originated in India.
Mexican Cream	Small, flesh is thick and white, soft seeds in small cavity. Sweet.	Originated in Mexico.
Red Indian	Small to medium, flesh is thick and red, few seeds. Sprightly flavor, minimal muskiness. Excellent quality.	Originated in Florida.
Ruby	Medium, red flesh. Sweet, pleasant flavor. High quality.	Originated in Florida.
7199	Medium, flesh is thin and pink, few seeds. Sweet, slightly musky.	Originated in Florida.
6363	Large, flesh is thick and white, few seeds. Sweet, slightly musky.	Originated in Florida.
Supreme	Large, flesh is thick and white. Sweet. Good quality.	Originated in Florida.
Turnbull	Medium to large, white flesh, moderately seedy. Excellent flavor.	Tends to rot at flower end. Originated in Florida.
White Indian	Small to medium, flesh is thick and white, moderately seedy. Excellent, sprightly flavor.	Originated in Florida.
Juice Varieties		
Beaumont	Medium, white flesh, moderately seedy. Mildly acidic flavor.	Originated in Hawaii.
Blitch	Small, light pink flesh, many small seeds. Tart, pleasant flavor. Strong aroma.	
Ka Hua Kula	Medium, flesh is thick and pink, few seeds. Mildly acidic flavor.	Originated in Hawaii.
Patillo	Small, deep-pink flesh, small seeds. Mildly acidic flavor.	Originated in Florida.
Puerto Rico #2	Small to medium, flesh is thin and salmon, moderately seedy. Mildly acidic flavor.	Originated in Puerto Rico.

Kiwi Fruit

Kiwi fruit are becoming more popular every year. Although the first large commercial kiwi farms in the United States were planted just a short time ago, about 1970, this odd-looking, egg-shaped fruit with shimmering emerald green flesh and a delicious berry flavor has found a permanent home on American tables. The kiwi vine is also working its way into many American gardens. The vines are adaptable to a variety of climates, and close relatives of the kiwi with similar fruit (see page 55) are extremely hardy and extend kiwi fruit culture into the coldest northern regions. In addition to bearing delicious fruit, the vines also have attractive foliage and flowers and an interesting twining habit.

Kiwi fruit are borne on fast-growing deciduous vines that need heavy annual pruning to keep them productive and within bounds. It is not unusual for a healthy vine to cover an area 10 to 15 feet wide, 18 to 24 feet long, and 9 to 12 feet high.

The dark green leaves are round, 5 to 8 inches wide, and have fuzzy white undersides. The new growth is velvety brown. The yellowish white flowers are about an inch in diameter and borne in the leaf axils of the new shoots. The round to oblong fruit have a fuzzy brown, almost leathery skin enclosing soft, bright green flesh dotted with tiny, edible black seeds.

In the commercial orchard, kiwi vines are usually trained on wire trellises elevated 6 to 7 feet off the ground. In the garden, many more options are available. The vines can be trained over an arbor to shade a patio, tied to a trellis to soften a wall, or allowed to sprawl over a fence or pergola. With any of these methods, the fruit will hang from the vine in tantalizing clusters throughout the summer.

Adaptation

Kiwi vines can be grown in most areas of the United States where the temperature does not drop below 10° F. The flowers are susceptible to damage from late spring frosts and the fruit, which requires a growing season of at least 240 frost-free days to become sweet, can be damaged by hard frosts in the fall. The vines should be protected from strong winds; spring gusts can snap off new growth where it emerges from the canes. Kiwis are not recommended for Florida or the hot desert climates of the Southwest.

Most kiwi varieties have chilling requirements ranging from 400 to 800 hours, but low-chill varieties, such as 'Vincent', can be grown in mild areas with fewer than 100 hours of chilling. In areas with very mild winters the vines may retain their leaves all winter and fail to flower the following spring.

Common Name: Kiwi fruit, yang-tao, Chinese gooseberry.

Botanical Name: *Actinidia chinensis.*

Origin: China.

Growth Habit: Vigorous deciduous vine requiring trellis support.

Adaptation: Hardy to 10° F. Most varieties require 600 to 800 hours of chilling, but low-chill selections are available. Blossoms are susceptible to damage from spring frosts. The new growth is brittle and easily broken in strong winds. Not adapted to Florida.

Harvest Season: October and November. Available in markets the year around.

Begins Bearing: Within 3 to 4 years after planting for grafted and cutting-grown plants. Seedlings take at least 6 to 7 years.

Propagation: From cuttings and grafting.

Maintenance: High.

Pollination: Self-unfruitful. Male and female plants must be grown together for fruit production.

Suitability for Containers: For a short period or in a large box.

Landscape Quality: Excellent. Can be trained over an arbor for shade.

Nurseries: E, F, G, H, I, K, L, N, O, R, S, Y.

Information: 1, 2, 3, 7, 8, 9, 11, 13.

Kiwi fruit change from this bright green color to a darker green with a brownish tinge when they are mature.

Also, incompletely dormant vines do not respond well to pruning. Some growers have successfully induced dormancy by stripping the foliage from the plants or by withholding water, but these techniques are severe and should be used only as a last resort.

Pollination

Kiwi vines are either male or female; you need at least one of each for fruit production. Commercial growers plant one male surrounded by eight females with about 15 to 18 feet between plants, but a pair of vines usually supplies enough fruit for home gardeners. Don't prune the male vine until early summer, after the canes have flowered and the fruit has set on the female vine. It's important to select male and female plants that have the same chilling requirements so they break dormancy and flower together. Insects are largely responsible for pollination.

Propagation

Kiwi vines can be propagated under mist from dormant hardwood cuttings or semihardwood cuttings taken in July or August. Many nurseries also graft selected varieties onto seedling rootstocks in May or June. In mild-winter areas there appears to be no advantage to planting cutting-grown plants instead of grafted plants, but in cold climates cutting-grown plants are superior because if the top of the plant is killed by frost it can resprout from the roots and still be true to type.

Seedling plants have varied chilling requirements and don't bear fruit of dependable quality, so it is best to stick with grafted or cutting-grown plants. Seedlings also take much longer to bear fruit.

Site Selection and Planting

Kiwi fruit grow in full sun or partial shade. They prefer a well-drained soil that is rich in organic matter with a pH range between 5.5 and 7.0. Provide protection in windy areas. Kiwis do not tolerate salty soils.

Emerald kiwi slices add a jewel-like finishing touch to a variety of desserts.

Install a trellis or other support at planting time (see "Pruning," below). If you are planting just two vines, do not let the male and female intertwine, or pruning will be difficult. Instead, plant them 12 to 15 feet apart.

Kiwi vines can be planted bareroot or from containers.

Caring for Kiwi Vines

Watering The vigorous growth and abundant foliage of the kiwi vine call for plenty of soil moisture. Water deeply and frequently in a basin that extends 5 to 6 feet from the trunk. Water-stressed plants drop their leaves, exposing the fruit to sunburn. They also may not flower the following year. Keep the soil moist until harvest, but cut back on the water as fall approaches in order to encourage dormancy.

In parts of Southern California where hot, dry winds are common in the fall, mulch the ground under the entire canopy of the vine and keep it moist. This will, it is hoped, increase the humidity enough to prevent leaf drop.

Fertilizing The kiwi fruit is a vigorous plant and needs about 1 pound of actual nitrogen per year. Young vines are very sensitive to overfertilization, and need only one eighth to one quarter that amount. Spread the fertilizer evenly under the entire canopy. Late fertilization may delay dormancy, so don't fertilize after midsummer. Chelated micronutrients may be needed in some areas.

Pruning Kiwi vines must be pruned and trained carefully. Without pruning, the vines quickly become a fruitless jungle.

There are basically two training methods: the fruiting lateral method and the spur method. The one you choose will depend on how much room you have and how many plants you want to grow.

In the fruiting lateral method (preferred by most commercial growers), the vines are trained on a five-wire trellis supported 6 feet above the ground by posts topped with T-shaped arms. The fruiting canes develop from permanent arms (called cordons) and are trained along the trellis wires.

The spur method is preferable where space is limited. In this case, the short fruiting spurs originate from the main trunk or permanent cordons. The canes that grow from these spurs each season are tied to a fence, wall, or trellis.

Both training techniques require a strong support. If you build a trellis, construct it with strong materials that will last a long time—kiwi fruit can remain productive for more than 40 years. Any wood that will be in direct contact with the soil should be pressure treated with wood preservatives.

Regardless of the training method you choose, let the young plants grow with minimal pruning for a year or two after planting. If a strong main trunk, more than ¼ inch in diameter, doesn't develop the first year, cut the vine back to two or three buds above the ground or graft union the following dormant season. In the spring train the most vigorous shoot up the trellis. During the training period the plant's energy should be directed into developing a strong trunk and arms or spurs.

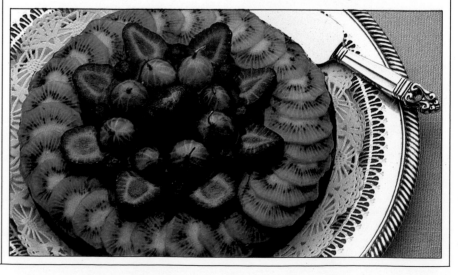

Training Kiwi Vines for Arbors

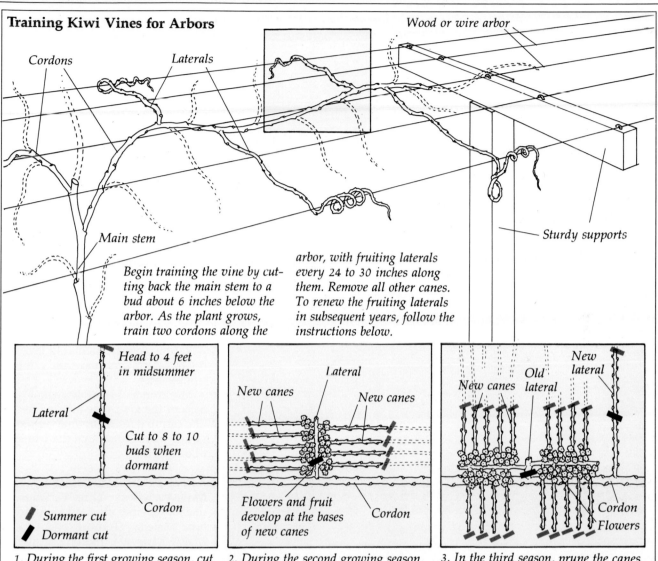

Cordons

Laterals

Wood or wire arbor

Main stem

Sturdy supports

Begin training the vine by cutting back the main stem to a bud about 6 inches below the arbor. As the plant grows, train two cordons along the arbor, with fruiting laterals every 24 to 30 inches along them. Remove all other canes. To renew the fruiting laterals in subsequent years, follow the instructions below.

Head to 4 feet in midsummer

Lateral

Cut to 8 to 10 buds when dormant

Cordon

▰ Summer cut
▮ Dormant cut

New canes

Lateral

New canes

Flowers and fruit develop at the bases of new canes

Cordon

New canes

Old lateral

New lateral

Cordon

Flowers

1. During the first growing season, cut the laterals to about 4 feet or to just beyond the outside of the arbor. During the winter, cut back laterals to 8 to 10 buds.

2. During the second growing season, after the vines flower, cut the new canes to 8 to 10 buds past the last blossom. During the winter, cut the laterals to just past the cane that bore the fruit the previous year.

3. In the third season, prune the canes as in the second season, and allow new laterals to develop between the old ones. During winter, remove any laterals that have fruited twice and replace as in step 1.

Spur-Pruning for Fences and Walls

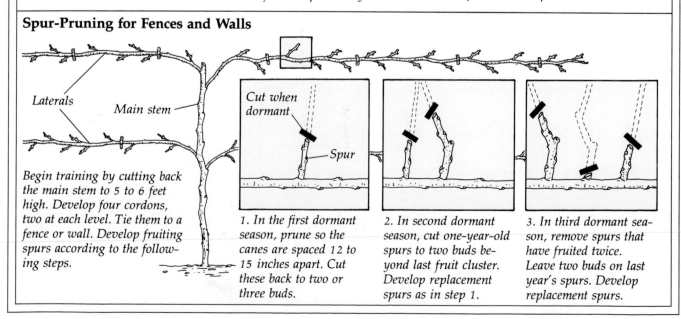

Laterals

Main stem

Cut when dormant

Spur

Begin training by cutting back the main stem to 5 to 6 feet high. Develop four cordons, two at each level. Tie them to a fence or wall. Develop fruiting spurs according to the following steps.

1. In the first dormant season, prune so the canes are spaced 12 to 15 inches apart. Cut these back to two or three buds.

2. In second dormant season, cut one-year-old spurs to two buds beyond last fruit cluster. Develop replacement spurs as in step 1.

3. In third dormant season, remove spurs that have fruited twice. Leave two buds on last year's spurs. Develop replacement spurs.

The twining growth of a kiwi vine shades a patio and will provide a delicious crop of fruit.

Prune the female vines during the dormant season. You will also need to prune them occasionally in the summer to remove vigorous shoots that are getting in the way or straying out of bounds.

Remove about half of the growth on male vines after they have finished blooming.

Pests and Diseases   Root-knot nematodes may limit yields, but kiwi vines are so vigorous and productive that the problem may never be noticed.

Oak root fungus infects kiwis in some California soils. Other soil-borne pathogens threaten only plants in poorly drained soils.

Various insects, including leaf roller, caterpillars, and scale can be troublesome.

The aroma of the foliage and bark of the kiwi vine affects cats like catnip does. They may uproot young plants or scratch the trunks of older vines.

Kiwi Fruit Varieties

Male Varieties   Three varieties of male kiwi vines are used as pollinators: 'Mateua', 'Tomuri', and 'Chico Male'. 'Mateua' is used most often because of its long blooming period. Although it usually blooms earlier than the female 'Monty' and 'Hayward' varieties, there is usually enough overlap for fruit set. When available, the late-blooming 'Tomari' pollinator can also be used to pollinate 'Monty' and either of the 'Hayward' varieties. 'Chico Male' is sometimes preferred as a pollinator for 'Chico Hayward'.

Female Varieties   See the chart at left for the most common varieties.

Harvest and Storage

Kiwi fruit is picked when still hard and ripened off the vine like a pear or avocado. The trick is to know when the fruit is ready to pick. A change of color from greenish brown to brown is a sign that the fruit is almost mature. Also, look for a few fruit beginning to soften on the vine. Pick the largest fruit first, giving the smaller ones a little more time to swell and sweeten. Fruit left on the vine too long

Female Kiwi Fruit Varieties

VARIETY	FRUIT DESCRIPTION	COMMENTS
Abbott	Small, early, round with long, soft, dense hairs. Similar to Allison.	Vigorous vine bears heavily, flowers early. Fruit small unless thinned. Medium chilling requirement.
Bruno	Midseason, oblong with dark brown bristly hairs.	Vigorous vines produce heavily; fruit must be thinned. Not for areas with short growing seasons. Medium chilling requirement.
Chico Hayward	Large, late, oblong, pale greenish brown with fine, silky hairs. Tends to produce some odd-shaped fruit.	Fruit quality excellent, indistinguishable from Hayward. Light crop; doesn't have to be thinned as much as others. Preferred commercial variety. High chilling requirement.
Hayward	Identical to 'Chico Hayward'.	Excellent quality. Fruit doesn't need to be thinned. High chilling requirement. Originated in New Zealand.
Monty	Small to medium, early, oblong.	Vigorous vine bears heavily. Fruit must be thinned. Flowers early. Medium chilling requirement. Low-quality fruit.
Tewi	Medium, early, oblong.	Moderate vigor. Flowers early. Fruit need to be thinned for good size. Low chilling requirement.
Vincent	Similar to 'Chico Hayward'.	Vigorous vine bears heavily. Flowers and ripens early. Fruit must be thinned. Low chilling requirement.

will soften and decay and will probably be eaten by birds. A light frost (31° F) will not damage the fruit, and may even improve its quality, but lower temperatures will make it inedible.

Kiwi fruit usually ripens in November in hot areas, or in December in cooler climates.

Kiwi fruit will soften in a few days when kept at room temperature. Unbruised mature fruit may be stored for up to six months in the refrigerator if the air circulation is good and they are kept away from other ripening fruits such as apples or bananas. Check the fruit often while it is in storage and remove any decaying pieces.

Kiwi Fruit Relatives

Several close relatives of the kiwi produce delicious fruit and are very hardy. The tara vine or hardy kiwi, *Actinidia arguta*, is reportedly hardy to -20° F. The plant is very similar to the kiwi fruit but the leaves are slightly longer and more pointed. As with the kiwi, male and female plants are required for pollination. The fruit has a kiwi flavor but is a little smaller and can be eaten skin and all. It ripens on the vine in areas with 200 frost-free days, but can be picked when still hard and ripened at room temperature in areas with shorter growing seasons.

The tara vine has attracted the attention of botanists and plant breeders around the world. American selections include 'Meader #1' and 'Geneva'.

Actinidia kolomikta is a slender, deciduous vine with variegated pink-and-white foliage. It is hardy to -20° to -30° F. The flowers are fragrant. The small (¾- to 1-inch-long) fruit ripen over an extended period, making them well suited for the home garden.

Kiwi Fruit at the Table

The kiwi fruit, when pared and sliced crosswise, adds a beautiful, jewel-like finishing touch to a variety of dishes. Thin slices on a tart of *pâte brisée* and pastry cream have a translucent emerald glow. The kiwi fruit is excellent with prosciutto or coppa as an hors d'oeuvre, in salads (both green and fruit), as a garnish for a delicate dish of chicken breasts in cream and Sauterne, and makes fine sorbets and jellies.

Litchi

A litchi tree in full fruit is a stunning sight. Large clusters of bright red fruit dangle among shiny, leathery, dark green leaves divided into four to eight leaflets. Litchis are also eye-catching in spring, when huge sprays of yellowish white flowers adorn the tree.

The fruit are encased within a brittle, warty shell. Inside this shell is a sweet, translucent, gelatinous delicacy that the Chinese have enjoyed for more than 2,000 years.

Litchi trees have full foliage and branch to the ground. Under ideal conditions they may reach 40 feet high, but they are usually much smaller. In some areas litchis have a tendency for alternate bearing.

These bright red litchi fruit are ready to be harvested.

Common Name: Litchi, leechee, lychee.
Botanical Name: *Litchi chinensis*.
Origin: Southern China.
Growth Habit: Slow-growing evergreen tree or large shrub to more than 30 feet high and equally wide under ideal conditions.
Adaptation: Has specific requirements for fruit production: hot, humid summers and cool winters. Trees are hardy to about 25° F.
Harvest Season: June through August.
Begins Bearing: Selected varieties usually begin bearing in 3 to 5 years. Seedlings take much longer, if they bear at all.
Propagation: Easiest by air-layering. Grafting is difficult. Seedlings produce unreliable fruit.
Maintenance: Moderate.
Pollination: Self-fruitful.
Suitability for Containers: For a short period or in a large box.
Landscape Quality: Excellent.
Nurseries: E, I, O, P, Q, U, Y.
Information: 1, 2, 8, 13, 14.

Adaptation

Litchis require seasonal temperature variations for best flowering and fruiting. Warm, humid summers are best for flowering and fruit development, and a certain amount of winter chilling is necessary for flower bud development. Varieties differ as to how much chilling they need, but most need between 100 and 200 hours between 32° and 45° F. Cool winters with low amounts of rainfall are ideal for litchis.

Litchi trees become more hardy as they age. Mature trees have survived temperatures as low as 25° F when fully hardened off. Young trees may be killed by a light frost.

Litchis are best adapted to parts of Hawaii and Florida, but they have also been grown successfully in frost-free coastal areas of California.

Propagation

Air-layering is the most common method of propagating litchis because grafting is difficult and seedlings are not reliable producers of quality fruit. Young plants propagated by air-layering should be grown in containers for one or two seasons before planting. This allows the root system to develop and increases the likelihood of successful transplanting. See page 86 for an illustration of air layering.

Pollination

Although litchi trees are usually self-fruitful, more male flowers are produced than female flowers. In rare cases trees may produce only male flowers and therefore won't set fruit.

Site Selection and Planting

Plant litchis in full sun and well-drained soil that is rich in organic matter. A soil pH between 5.5 and 7.5 is acceptable, but plants grow much better in soils with a ph at the low end of this range. Apply a thick layer of organic mulch to the soil after planting.

Caring for Litchi Trees

Watering The litchi will not tolerate standing water, but requires very moist soil, so water the tree regularly when it is growing actively. Litchi trees are very sensitive to damage from salts in the soil or in water. Leach the soil regularly in the Southwest.

Fertilizing Young trees tend to grow slowly, and many gardeners give them too much fertilizer in an attempt to push them along. Young trees should receive only light applications of a complete fertilizer, if anything at all. Mature trees are heavier feeders and should be fertilized regularly from spring to late summer. Use fertilizers formulated for acid-loving plants such as rhododendrons and azaleas. Chelated iron and soil sulfur may be necessary soil amendments in areas with alkaline soils.

Pruning Prune young trees to establish a strong, permanent structure for easy harvest. After that, removing crossing or damaged branches is all that is necessary, although the trees can be pruned more heavily to control size.

Pests and Diseases Mites, scale, and aphids occasionally infest litchis. Fruit splitting is usually caused by fluctuating soil moisture levels. Mold often grows in the cracked fruit, but you can avoid this problem by watering regularly.

Birds are often attracted to litchis, eating both the immature and the ripe fruit. Cover plants with protective netting if you find you are losing too many fruit to the birds.

Two varieties of Litchi chinensis*: 'Sweet Cliff' (right), and 'Brewster' (below)*

Litchi Varieties

VARIETY	FRUIT DESCRIPTION*	COMMENTS
Amboina	Medium, bright red, borne in clusters of 6 to 20. Ripens April to May.	Slow-growing tree; bears regularly in warm climates.
Bengal	Large, bright red, borne in clusters of 8 to 30. Large seed. Ripens in June.	Large, very vigorous tree. Easy to grow.
Brewster	Medium, bright red, spiny, borne in clusters of 6 to 20. Large seed. Ripens June to July.	Large, vigorous, upright tree.
Groff	Small, dull red, spiny, borne in clusters of 20 to 40. Small seed. Ripens August to September.	Latest-ripening variety. Upright tree.
Hap Ip	Medium, dark red, smooth, borne in clusters of 15 to 25. Large seed. Ripens in July.	Slow growing, compact tree with spreading branches.
Kwai Mi (Kuei Wei)	Small, bright red, slightly spiny, borne in clusters of 15 to 30. Large seed. Ripens May to June.	Large, spreading tree with brittle branches.
Mauritius	Medium, bright red, smooth, borne in clusters of 15 to 30. Large seed. Ripens May to June.	Vigorous, spreading tree with weak branches. Cold-sensitive.
No Mai Tsz (No Mai Tze, No Mai Chi)	Medium, bright reddish yellow, borne in clusters of 10 to 25. Brittle skin, small seed. Ripens in July.	Poor in Hawaii. Slow-growing, spreading tree.
Pat Po Hung	Small, bright red, borne in clusters of 10 to 25. Thin, rough skin. Ripens May to June.	Slow-growing tree with sprawling branches.
Sweet Cliff	Small, pinkish yellow to red, borne in clusters of 4 to 8. Seed small to medium. Ripens in June.	Recommended for Florida. Poor in alkaline soils. Small, slow-growing tree.

*Harvest dates are for Florida and Hawaii. The fruit will ripen 3 to 4 months later in California.

Harvest and Storage

Fruit must be allowed to ripen fully on the tree. You will probably have to do some experimenting to determine at what stage you like the fruit best. Fruit of each variety has a characteristic color change as it ripens. Overly mature fruit darken in color and lose their luster. The flavor lacks the richness associated with a certain amount of acidity. Immature fruit are very acidic.

To harvest, snip off entire fruit clusters, keeping a short piece of stem attached. Be careful to leave the fruit casing intact, because damaged fruit will decay quickly.

Litchis can be stored for up to five weeks in the refrigerator. They can also be frozen or dried (see "Litchis at the Table," below). Litchis will begin to deteriorate within three days at room temperature.

Litchis at the Table

Fresh litchis are delicious when combined with other tropical fruit in salads. They can also be cooked in a sweet syrup and canned. Another easy way to handle a big harvest of litchis is to dry them.

Dried Litchi Nuts

Pick the litchis without breaking off the stem end. Remove them from the shell. Spread the shelled nuts on a tray one layer thick. Place them in the sun, in a gas oven with only the pilot light on, or in an electric oven set at the lowest temperature. Turn fruit several times each day so they dry evenly. If drying outside, do not let the litchis get wet; cover or bring them indoors at night.

The time it takes for the litchis to dry properly varies according to the drying method, but it usually takes several days. Properly dried litchis are shriveled but moist, light brown, and delicious. They can be stored for up to a year.

Loquat

Loquats are easy-to-grow plants with boldly textured foliage and clusters of small, orangeish yellow fruit 1 to 2 inches in diameter. Each fruit contains three to five large seeds surrounded by sweet, tangy, and aromatic flesh. This flesh may be orange, yellow, or white, depending on the variety.

Loquat trees are often grown as ornamentals. Their large, prominently veined leaves contrast well with plants having smaller, softer leaves. The undersides of the leaves are light green and often covered with a soft down. The new growth is sometimes tinged with red. Mature trees are roundheaded and can be used to shade a patio. Loquats also make attractive espaliers.

Small, white, fragrant flowers are borne at the ends of the branches in the fall or early winter. Before they open, the flower clusters have an unusual woolly texture. In full bloom the trees will be alive with bees.

Adaptation

Loquats produce the best fruit in areas with mild winters and mild summers. Although the tree is quite hardy, temperatures near 28° F. will usually damage the flowers and ripening fruit. Prolonged high summer temperatures can inhibit flowering. Intense heat and sunlight during the winter usually result in sunburned fruit. The white-fleshed varieties are better adapted to cool coastal areas. The varieties with yellow flesh need more warmth to produce sweet fruit.

Common Name: Loquat, Japanese medlar, Japanese plum.

Botanical Name: *Eriobotrya japonica*.

Origin: China and Japan.

Growth Habit: Large evergreen shrub or tree to 25 feet high and 30 feet wide under ideal conditions.

Adaptation: Foliage is hardy to 20° F, but mature trees have survived at 12° F. The fruit and flowers can be damaged by hard frosts. Widely grown in the West and Southeast.

Harvest Season: January to May in Southeast. March to June in West.

Begins Bearing: In 3 to 4 years.

Propagation: Easily grown from seed, but the fruit quality will be unpredictable. Selected varieties are usually grafted onto seedling rootstocks.

Maintenance: Low.

Pollination: Self-fruitful.

Suitability for Containers: Well-suited.

Landscape Quality: Good.

Nurseries: E, I, O, P, Q, S, U, Y.

Information: 1, 2, 13, 14.

Loquat: Eriobotrya japonica

Propagation

Loquat varieties selected for quality fruit are usually propagated by shield-budding or side-veneer grafts. Small plants can be cleft-grafted. Many nurseries sell seedling-grown plants for use as ornamentals, but these trees seldom produce quality fruit.

Site Selection and Planting

Loquats will grow best in full sun but also do well in partial shade. They will adapt to almost any well-drained soil.

Caring for Loquat Trees

Watering   Loquat trees are drought tolerant, but they will produce higher-quality fruit with regular, deep watering. The trees will not tolerate standing water.

Fertilizing   Loquats benefit from regular, light applications of nitrogen fertilizers, but too much nitrogen will reduce flowering. Fertilize two or three times from spring to early summer. Do not fertilize after midsummer.

Pruning   Loquats get along fine with a minimum of pruning. To make the tree more attractive, occasionally remove crossing branches and thin any dense growth to let light into the center of the tree. The tree also responds well to more severe pruning and can be trained as an espalier.

Pests and Diseases   In California, loquats have few problems. In Florida, the Caribbean fruit fly is a serious pest.

In areas with late spring and summer rains or high humidity, the trees may get fire blight. To control fire blight, remove the scorched-looking branches, cutting well into live wood. Sterilize the shears between cuts by dipping them in a 10 percent solution of household bleach or in undiluted rubbing alchohol. Burn the prunings or seal them in a plastic bag before disposal.

Anthracnose may also infect loquats.

Harvest and Storage

Loquats should be allowed to ripen fully before they are harvested. The fruit develops a distinctive color (depending on the variety) and begins to soften when ripe. Ripe fruit may be stored in the refrigerator for one to two weeks.

Loquats at the Table

Loquats are delicious when eaten fresh but can also be dried or used to make jams, jellies, preserves, and the following spicy sauce.

Spicy Loquat Sauce

    4 quarts fresh loquats
       (6½ pounds)
       Ground cinnamon
       Ground nutmeg
       Sugar (optional)

1. Wash loquats; halve fruit and discard seeds. Place in kettle, add water to partially cover. Cover kettle and bring water to a boil. Boil gently until fruit is tender, about 30 minutes. Remove from heat and let cool. Purée fruit by pressing it through a food mill, colander, or sieve. Add ground cinnamon and nutmeg to taste. Add a little sugar, if desired.

2. Place the mixture in a saucepan and bring it to a boil. Pour into hot, sterilized jars. Seal and process in boiling water for 15 minutes. Serve the sauce chilled on roasts, as a substitute for applesauce, or as a topping for ice cream.

Makes 3 cups.

Loquat Varieties

VARIETY	FRUIT DESCRIPTION	COMMENTS
Advance	Large, oblong, yellow skin, white flesh. Good quality. Ripens midseason.	Self-unfruitful. Pollinate with 'Gold Nugget'.
Bartow (Fletcher White)	Pale yellow skin, white flesh. Good quality. Ripens midseason.	
Big Jim	Large, oblong, pale orange skin, orange flesh. Very sweet. Ripens late in season.	Vigorous, upright growth.
Bradenton (Hastings)	Large, oblong, pale yellow skin. Ripens midseason. Excellent quality.	Vigorous, upright tree.
Champagne	Light yellow skin, white flesh. Good tart flavor. Ripens late.	Self-unfruitful.
Fletcher Red	Large, oblong, thick orange-red skin, orange-red flesh. Excellent flavor. Ripens midseason.	Slow-growing, upright tree. Fruit stores well.
Gold Nugget	Round, deep-orange skin, yellow-orange flesh. Good sweet-tart flavor. Ripens late.	Vigorous, upright growth.
Hardee	Round, pale yellow skin. Fair quality. Ripens midseason.	Vigorous tree.
Oliver	Round, deep-yellow skin. Excellent flavor. Ripens midseason.	Vigorous tree.
Premier	Oblong, pale yellow skin. Very sweet. Ripens early.	Dwarf, slow-growing tree.
Ses 2	Oblong, pale yellow skin. Good flavor. Ripens midseason.	Vigorous tree.
Tanaka	Large, oblong, deep-yellow skin, yellow-orange flesh. Very good, sweet-tart flavor. Ripens late.	Vigorous tree.
Thales	Round, yellow skin, yellow-orange flesh. Good, sweet-tart flavor. Ripens midseason.	Self-pollinating. Vigorous tree.
Wolfe	Oblong, pale yellow skin. Excellent flavor. Ripens midseason.	Excellent for cooking.

Experiment with your harvests. Many subtropical fruits can be preserved, producing treats such as these dried loquats. Halved loquats take 2 to 3 days to dry in the sun, 16 to 36 hours in a dehydrator.

Macadamia

There are two species of macadamia that produce nuts with edible kernels. The smooth-shelled macadamia, *Macadamia integrifolia*, is the species grown commercially in Hawaii and marketed as the macadamia nut. Its common name describes the smooth, very hard seed coat. This shell is enclosed in a green husk that splits open as the nut matures. The creamy white kernel contains up to 80 percent oil and 4 percent sugar. When roasted, it develops a uniform color and texture and a delicious flavor.

Smooth-shelled macadamias develop from creamy white flowers borne in clusters 6 to 12 inches long. The trees have shiny, leathery, deep green leaves ranging from 5 to 10 inches long, arranged in

Common Name: Macadamia, Queensland nut, Australian nut.

Botanical name: *Macadamia* species.

Origin: Coastal rain forests of Australia.

Growth Habit: Evergreen trees reaching 30 to 40 feet high and almost as wide.

Adaptation: Mature trees can survive temperatures as low as 24° F, but young trees can be killed by a light frost. Consistently high summer temperatures reduce yields.

Harvest Season: Late fall to spring.

Begins Bearing: Grafted varieties begin bearing within 4 to 6 years. Seedlings may take 10 to 12 years.

Propagation: Grafting used most often. Cuttings and air-layering are also successful. Seedlings are unreliable.

Maintenance: Low.

Pollination: Self-fruitful, but planting two different varieties often results in higher yields.

Suitability for Containers: For a short period or in a large box.

Landscape Quality: Good.

Nurseries: E, I, O, S, Y.

Information: 1, 2, 6, 8, 13.

whorls of three. The juvenile leaves of seedlings are usually spiny, but the leaf margins of older trees are most often smooth.

Macadamia tetraphylla is usually grown as a rootstock for the smooth-skinned macadamia. Its rough, pebbled seed coat accounts for its common name, the rough-shelled macadamia. The quality of the kernel of the rough-skinned macadamia is more variable than that of the smooth-skinned macadamia. Oil content ranges from 65 percent to 75 percent and sugar content ranges from 6 percent to 8 percent. These characteristics result in variable color and texture when the nut is roasted, making the rough-skinned macadamia less desirable commercially. It is, however, well suited to the home garden and has been planted for commercial production in California. The flowers are pink and borne in clusters up to 15 inches long. The leaves are deep green, 8 to 20 inches long, and arranged in whorls of four. The edges of the leaves are spiny or toothed, and the new growth has an attractive pink tinge.

Adaptation

Macadamias are ideally suited to a mild, frost-free climate with abundant rainfall distributed evenly throughout the year, such as the climate found in parts of Hawaii. Both species, however, will also grow well in the coastal areas of California and in Southern Florida. Also, macadamia varieties respond differently depending on where they are grown. Varieties that grow well in Hawaii may not do well in California or Florida. The California Macadamia Society (see page 94) and your local cooperative extension agent are good sources of information on what varieties are best for your area.

Mature macadamia trees are fairly hardy, tolerating temperatures as low as 24° F, but the flower clusters are usually killed at 28° F. Young macadamia trees can be killed by light frosts.

The brittle branches of the macadamia can be damaged by the wind, particularly when laden with a heavy crop of nuts.

Above: *Macadamia 'Beaumont' draped with lacy flowers.* Top right: *Smooth-shelled macadamia:* Macadamia integrifolia.

Macadamia nuts and mangoes combine to make a light, flavorful stuffing for chicken. See page 61 for the recipe.

Macadamia Varieties

VARIETY	NUT DESCRIPTION	COMMENTS
Varieties for Hawaii*		
Hinde	Large nut, fair-quality kernel sticks to shell. Medium-thick shell.	Upright tree.
Ikaika	Medium nut, poor-quality kernel. Medium-thick shell.	Round, conical, vigorous tree. Bears early in year.
Kakea	Large nut, excellent-quality kernel. Medium-thick shell. Productive.	Upright tree is difficult to graft. Fairly cold-tolerant.
Kau	Large nut. Medium-thick shell.	Upright, conical tree tolerates cold.
Keaau	Small nut, very high-quality kernel. Thin shell.	Upright, conical tree.
Keauhou	Large nut, fair kernel quality. Medium-thick shell.	Spreading, cold-sensitive tree.
Makai	Very large nut, good kernel quality. Medium-thick shell.	Spreading, cold-sensitive tree.
Mauka	Medium-sized nut. Medium-thick shell.	Spreading, cold-tolerant tree.
Pahala	Medium-sized nut, good-quality kernel. Medium-thick shell.	Very upright tree.
Varieties for California**		
Beaumont	Good quality, medium-thick shell.	Nuts ripen over a long period. Excellent home garden tree. Hybrid between smooth-shelled and rough-shelled species. Upright habit.
Burdick	Fair quality, thick shell.	Usually used as a rootstock.
Cate	Excellent quality, thin shell.	Widely planted commercially. Nuts ripen over 2-month period. Spreading tree.
Elimbah	Good quality, thin shell.	Ripens late. Upright tree is difficult to graft.

These are selections of Macadamia integrifolia. **Most of these are selections of* Macadamia tetraphylla.

Propagation

Macadamias are easily grown from seed, but the seedlings may take 8 to 12 years to bear a crop and the quality of the nuts is unpredictable.

Grafting is the most common method of producing nursery trees. Seedling rootstocks, about ⅜ inch in diameter, are grafted to selected varieties with a side-veneer or side-wedge graft. The scion wood should be girdled 6 to 8 weeks before being cut and grafted (see page 86).

Macadamias can also be propagated from softwood cuttings or by air-layering. Cutting-grown trees will need staking when young.

Site Selection and Planting

Full sun is best, but in windy or hot climates, provide protection and partial shade. A deep, rich soil with a pH of 5.5 to 6.5 is ideal. Macadamias will not tolerate soil or water with high salt concentrations. In areas with low annual rainfall, leach the soil regularly.

Caring for Macadamia Trees

Watering   Macadamias can withstand periods of drought, but the harvests will be small and of low quality. Water regularly and deeply during dry periods.

Fertilizing   Because macadamias grow slowly, they do not require large quantities of nitrogen fertilizer. Micronutrient deficiencies are common in some areas, particularly southern Florida, but these can be corrected with chelated sprays.

Pruning   Prune young trees to encourage strong branching. Mature trees need little pruning other than removing crossing or damaged branches. Heavy pruning drastically reduces yields.

Pests and Diseases   Few pests or diseases cause serious problems to macadamias in home gardens. Occasionally, thrips or mites may be troublesome. Anthracnose may infect leaves and nuts in humid climates.

Harvest and Storage

Mature macadamias will fall to the ground from late fall to spring. Gather them as soon as possible and remove the husks immediately. To ease the harvest, place a tarp under the tree and give the branches a gentle shake to dislodge the mature nuts.

Harvested nuts should be air-dried at temperatures not exceeding 110° F. They can be stored for six to eight months in a cool, dry area.

When the nuts are dry, remove the shells with a nutcracker.

Smooth-shelled macadamias can be dry-roasted at 300° F for 18 to 20 minutes or roasted in refined coconut oil for the same time. Roast rough-shelled macadamias at 275° F for 12 to 15 minutes.

Salt the roasted macadamias and store in airtight jars at 40° to 65° F.

Macadamia Nuts at the Table

Macadamias are excellent raw or roasted. They can be used in almost any recipe calling for nuts, including stuffings, fruit salads, breads, cakes, and pies. Crushed macadamia nuts are an excellent topping for baked fish or meat and combine very well with coconut milk in sauces.

Chicken With Macadamia-Mango Stuffing

- ½ cup chopped macadamia nuts
- ½ cup white seedless grapes or golden seedless raisins
- 2 mangoes, peeled, seeded, and cut into small pieces (1½ cups)
- ¼ cup finely chopped onion
- 2 tablespoons white wine
- 1 tablespoon brown sugar
- 1 tablespoon soy sauce
- 1 whole chicken (3 to 3½ lbs)
   Vegetable oil
   Salt and pepper

1. Preheat oven to 350° F. In a medium bowl combine macadamias, grapes, mangoes, onion, wine, brown sugar, and soy sauce; mix thoroughly.

2. Remove giblets from cavity of chicken and stuff chicken with macadamia mixture. Truss chicken. Rub chicken with oil; sprinkle with salt and pepper to taste. Place chicken in a roasting pan and bake, uncovered, until done, about 1 hour. When done, the juices will run clear when you pierce the thigh with a fork.

Serves 4 or 5.

Mango

The mango is the apple of the tropics. For many years, mangoes have been one of the most commonly eaten fruits in tropical countries around the world. Mangoes are also becoming increasingly popular in America, where they are available in supermarkets almost the year around.

Mangoes vary in size, shape, and color. They can be round, oblong, or kidney shaped. Sometimes the fruit has a small, pointed beak. They can weigh as little as 4 to 5 ounces or as much as 2 pounds. The skin color can be green, yellow, red, or purple, but usually it is a combination of several shades. The fibrous flesh is yellow to orange and when perfectly ripe, also has the texture of a peach. The flavor also resembles that of the peach, but it also has a distinctive tropical sweetness.

Mango trees make handsome landscape specimens and shade trees. The leaves are long, narrow, and a lustrous deep green. The new growth, which comes out in flushes, is often tinged with red. The fragrant yellow-to-red flowers are borne in terminal sprays. Although each flower cluster may have hundreds of blooms, only a few will set fruit. As a result, the fruit dangle at the ends of interesting stringlike stalks.

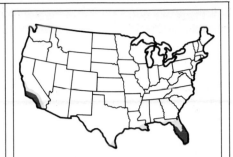

Common Name: Mango.
Botanical Name: *Mangifera indica.*
Origin: India and Southeast Asia.
Growth Habit: Evergreen tree reaching 50 feet under ideal conditions. Usually spreading to 30 feet but tree shape differs according to variety.
Adaptation: Best adapted to frost-free climates of Florida, Hawaii, and Southern California.
Harvest Season: Varies by area: May to July in Florida and Hawaii; fall to winter in California.
Begins Bearing: Grafted trees begin bearing in 2 to 3 years. Seedlings take 4 to 5 years.
Propagation: Some varieties grow true to type from seed. Others are grafted or budded.
Maintenance: Low.
Pollination: Self-fruitful.
Suitability for Containers: Unsuitable.
Landscape Quality: Excellent.
Nurseries: E, I, O, P, Q, S, U, Y.
Information: 1, 2, 13, 14.

Mango: Mangifera indica 'Keitt', *a variety for Florida.*

There are two types of mangoes: Indian and Indo-Chinese. Indian mangoes usually have brightly colored fruit, are susceptible to anthracnose, and produce monoembryonic seeds, which do not grow true to type. Indian mangoes are the type most often grown commercially in Florida. Indo-Chinese mangoes usually do not develop brightly colored fruit, but the trees are resistant to anthracnose. Indo-Chinese mangoes are also usually polyembryonic, meaning that most of the seedlings are identical to the parent plant.

Some mangoes do not fall clearly into either the Indian or the Indo-Chinese types. These naturally occurring seedlings are found in the tropics. Some of these, such as 'Turpentine', 'Number 11', and 'Julie', are named, cultivated varieties.

Most mangoes have a tendency to bear heavily in alternate years. To minimize alternate bearing, thin the fruit and fertilize more heavily in a heavy crop year.

Adaptation

Mangoes should be grown in frost-free climates. Flowers and small fruit can be killed if temperatures drop below 40° F, even if only for a short period. Young trees may be seriously damaged if the temperature drops below 30° F, but mature trees may withstand very short periods of temperatures as low as 25° F.

Mangoes must have warm, dry weather to set fruit. In California the first bloom of the season usually occurs during the cool, wet spring weather and results in poor fruit set. Later in the summer the second growth flush and bloom produce a crop that ripens in the fall and winter.

Pollination

Mangoes are self-fruitful, but the amount of fruit set depends largely on warm temperatures, low humidity, and the activity of pollinating insects. Wet, humid weather favors anthracnose and poor fruit set. Also, if the temperature falls below 55° F, insect activity is drastically reduced.

Propagation

Indo-Chinese mangoes have polyembryonic seeds, which produce two or more seedlings from each seed. Because most of these seedlings are identical to the parent, Indo-Chinese mangoes are commonly grown from seed.

To grow mangoes from seed, remove the husk and plant the seed (before it dries out) with the hump at soil level. Transplant the seedlings carefully, making sure not to sever the taproot.

Although most Indo-Chinese seedlings are true to type, some may be quite different from the parent, so for best results plant grafted or budded trees. If you want to graft your own trees, do it when the tree is in a growth flush. Side-wedge or side-veneer grafts are commonly used, but whip or cleft grafts can be used on larger plants. Many Florida nurseries also use shield- or chip-budding.

Site Selection and Planting

Plant mangoes in full sun and well-drained soil. A soil pH between 5.5 and 7.5 is preferred. When planting mangoes, take care not to damage the taproot.

Caring for Mango Trees

Watering   Mangoes require consistent moisture if they are to produce high-quality fruit. Water regularly in areas with low annual rainfall.

Fertilizing   Mango trees require regular applications of nitrogen fertilizer to promote healthy growth flushes and flower production; follow the feeding program recommended for citrus (see page 31). Chelated micronutrients, especially iron, are also often necessary.

Pruning   Healthy trees require little pruning, although pruning to stimulate new growth promotes uniform annual bearing. Removing some flower clusters during a heavy bloom year may also alleviate alternate bearing. Mangoes may be pruned to control size in late winter or early spring without a loss of fruit.

Pests and Diseases   Fungal dis-

Mango Varieties for Florida

VARIETY	FRUIT DESCRIPTION	COMMENTS
Adams	Small, red, fiberless. Ripens June to July.	Upright, slightly spreading tree. Susceptible to anthracnose.
Carrie	Medium, green and yellow, fiberless. Ripens June to July.	Small tree. Susceptible to anthracnose.
Earlygold	Medium, pink and yellow, fiberless. Mostly seedless. Ripens May to June.	Upright tree, light producer. Resists anthracnose.
Florigon	Medium, yellow, fiberless. Ripens May to July.	Upright, rounded, very productive tree. Moderately resistant to anthracnose.
Irwin	Medium, red, fiberless. Small seed. Ripens June to July.	Small tree. Susceptible to anthracnose.
Keitt	Large, green and pink, firm. Small seed. Ripens August to September.	Long, arching branches. Moderately resistant to anthracnose.
Kent	Large, green, red, and yellow, fiberless. Small seed. Ripens July to August.	Upright tree. Susceptible to anthracnose.
Osteen	Large, pink and red, almost fiberless. Ripens July to September.	Resists anthracnose.
Palmer	Large, red and yellow, almost fiberless. Ripens July to August.	Open, upright tree. Susceptible to anthracnose.
Parvin	Large, pink and red, almost fiberless. Ripens August to October.	Light producer. Resists anthracnose.
Ruby	Small, red, fiberless. Ripens July to August.	Upright, open, very productive tree. Susceptible to anthracnose.
Saigon	Small, green and yellow, fiberless. Ripens May to July.	Upright, rounded tree. Resists anthracnose.
Sensation	Medium, pink and red, some fiber. Small seed. Ripens July to August.	Moderately open tree. Tends to bear in alternate years. Susceptible to anthracnose.
Tommy Atkins	Large, red and yellow, firm. Small seed. Ripens June to July.	Dense, rounded tree. Moderately resistant to anthracnose.
Van Dyke	Medium, red and yellow, almost fiberless. Ripens July to August.	Open tree. Moderately resistant to anthracnose.

eases, including anthracnose, powdery mildew, and scab, can be serious problems in Florida and Hawaii. Consult your local cooperative extension office for preventive measures. Mites, thrips, and scale can be occasional problems. Mexican, Mediterranean, and Oriental fruit flies may be serious pests in Hawaii and in the Southeastern United States.

Harvest and Storage

Mango fruit matures 100 to 150 days after flowering. The fruit will take less time to ripen and will have the best flavor if allowed to ripen on the tree. Ripe fruit turns the characteristic color of the variety and begins to soften to the touch, much like a peach. Unripe fruit tastes like turpentine.

Mature, well-colored fruit can be picked firm and ripened at room temperature or stored for 20 to 25 days at cool temperatures. Do not store at a temperature below 55° F.

Mangoes at the Table

Despite the bothersome woody seed that clings to the meat, mangoes can be easily cut into large chunks of ambrosial flesh, provided the fruit is properly ripe and your knife is razor sharp.

To peel and seed a mango, make four longitudinal cuts in the skin and remove the sections of the peel as you would peel a banana. Then cut the flesh in slices parallel to the seed. Eat the slices out-of-hand, use them in an artful duck and mango salad, or let them marinate in Sauterne and lime juice and serve chilled as a superb dessert.

A surfeit of underripe mangoes goes well in duck or pork stews. Ripe mangoes are delicious in sweet breads, ice cream, sorbets, tarts, and chutneys.

Mango Leather

- 15 mangoes, puréed (about 8 cups)
- 1½ cups sugar
- 2 tablespoons ascorbic acid (available at pharmacies)
- 2 teaspoons cream of tartar

1. Combine mango purée, sugar, ascorbic acid, and cream of tartar in a saucepan and cook over high heat, stirring constantly to prevent burning. Allow the mixture to boil, stirring constantly, until slightly thickened, about 2 minutes. Remove from heat, and let cool.

2. Cover 6 cookie sheets or trays with plastic wrap, taping the edges to the bottoms of the sheets. Spread 1¼ cups of the mixture in a 14- by 10-inch rectangle on each cookie sheet (about ⅛ inch thick). Cover with cheesecloth and place in the sun. Dry until leathery. (This may take 2 or 3 days.) Do not allow trays to get wet; bring them inside at night.

3. Once leather is dry, remove cheesecloth and roll up leather in the plastic wrap. Will keep in the refrigerator for up to 6 months.

Makes 6 sheets of leather.

Mango: Mangifera indica *'Tommy Atkins', a variety for Florida.*

Mango Varieties for Hawaii

VARIETY	FRUIT DESCRIPTION	COMMENTS
Ah Ping	Large, yellow and orange, fiberless. Small seed. Ripens in July.	Upright tree. Susceptible to anthracnose.
Edwards	Large, dark yellow, fiberless. Small seed. Ripens June to July.	Spreading tree bears lightly. Susceptible to anthracnose.
Fairchild	Small, yellow, almost fiberless. Medium to large seed. Ripens in July.	Spreading tree bears lightly. Resists anthracnose.
Georgiana	Small, yellow with crimson blush, fiberless. Large seed. Ripens June to July.	Upright tree. Susceptible to anthracnose.
Gouveia	Large, maroon, fiberless. Small seed. Ripens in August.	Upright tree. Susceptible to anthracnose.
Joe Welch	Large, yellow, fiberless. Small seed. Ripens in July.	Productive, spreading tree. Susceptible to anthracnose.
Julie	Small, dark green and red, some fiber. Ripens August to September.	Small tree. Susceptible to anthracnose.
Ono	Small, yellow and purple, fiberless. Ripens in July.	Upright tree. Susceptible to anthracnose.
Pairi	Small, green and yellow, fiberless. Ripens in July.	Spreading tree bears lightly. Susceptible to anthracnose.
Smith	Medium to large, yellow with crimson blush, fiberless. Moderately large seed. Ripens July to August.	Spreading tree. Susceptible to anthracnose.
Zill	Small, yellow and crimson, fiberless. Small seed. Ripens June to July.	Dome-shaped tree. Susceptible to anthracnose.

Mango Chutney

- 1 cup distilled white vinegar
- 1 cup water
- 2 large onions, chopped (3 cups)
- 1 large clove garlic
- 10 cups pared, chopped, slightly green mango (13 to 15 mangoes; 7½ pounds)
- 1 cup granulated sugar
- 1 cup brown sugar, packed
- 1 cup slivered almonds
- ½ cup dark seedless raisins
- ½ cup dried currants
- 1½ teaspoons cumin seed
- 1 teaspoon *each* salt, curry powder, ground ginger, and dry mustard
- ½ teaspoon ground allspice
- ½ teaspoon cayenne pepper

1. Combine vinegar, water, onion, and garlic in a large kettle; bring to a boil. Boil 5 minutes. Remove and discard garlic clove.

2. Add mango, granulated and brown sugar, almonds, raisins, currants, cumin, salt, curry powder, ginger, mustard, allspice, and cayenne; return to boil. Continue boiling gently until the chutney thickens, about 30 minutes. Ladle into hot, sterilized jars and seal. Process for 15 minutes in a boiling water bath.

Makes 10 half-pints.

Mango: Mangifera indica 'Manila', *a variety for California.*

Mango Varieties for California

VARIETY	FRUIT DESCRIPTION	COMMENTS
Aloha	Small to large, red, almost fiberless. Small seed. Ripens November to December.	Spreading tree bears lightly. Susceptible to anthracnose.
Edgehill	Small to medium, green with red blush, almost fiberless. Ripens December to February.	Upright tree. Susceptible to anthracnose.
Kenny	Small, yellow, green, and pink, fiberless. Ripens October to November.	Rounded tree bears lightly. Susceptible to anthracnose.
Manila	Small, yellow, fiberless. Small seed. Ripens October to December.	Bushy plant. Polyembryonic seed. Susceptible to anthracnose.
Pina	Small, yellow and orange, almost fiberless. Ripens November to December.	Upright tree. Polyembryonic seed. Susceptible to anthracnose.
Reliable	Small to large, red and yellow, almost fiberless. Small seed. Ripens December to January.	Dome-shaped tree. Susceptible to anthracnose.
Surprise	Small to large, red and yellow, fiberless. Small seed. Ripens October to December.	Upright tree. Susceptible to anthracnose.
T-1	Medium to large, red, yellow, and green, fiberless. Small seed. Ripens December to January.	Upright, rounded tree. Susceptible to anthracnose.
Thomson	Small to medium, yellow, fiberless. Small seed. Ripens December to January.	Polyembryonic seed. Spreading tree. Susceptible to anthracnose.
Villasenor	Medium, light green with pink blush, fiberless. Small seed. Ripens December to January.	Spreading tree. Moderately resistant to anthracnose.
20222 (Winters)	Small to medium, red and yellow, fiberless. Ripens October to November.	Polyembryonic seed. Dome-shaped tree bears lightly. Susceptible to anthracnose.

Papaya

The papaya is an unbranched, single-stemmed herb that grows to a height of 6 to 20 feet. Its deeply lobed, dark green leaves have a boldly tropical look and reach 2 feet wide under ideal conditions.

There are three types of papayas: Hawaiian (*Carica papaya*), Mexican (*Carica pubescens*), and babaco (*Carica pentagona*). The Hawaiian varieties are the papayas commonly found in supermarkets. These pear-shaped fruit generally weigh about 1 pound and have a yellow skin when ripe. The flesh is bright orange or pinkish, depending on variety, with small black seeds clustered in the center. 'Solo', the most common variety, has orange flesh. 'Sunrise' has light pink flesh. Both varieties have a very pleasant, sweet flavor. Hawaiian papayas are easier to harvest because the plants seldom grow taller than 8 feet.

Mexican papayas are much larger than the Hawaiian types. They

Common Name: Papaya.

Botanical Name: *Carica* species.

Origin: Central America.

Growth Habit: Upright perennial herb reaching 6 to 20 feet high.

Adaptation: Frost-free climates of California, Florida, and Hawaii. Must have warm weather all year.

Harvest Season: Within 3 to 4 months after pollination in warm climates. About twice as long in cool climates.

Begins Bearing: Often within a year of planting.

Propagation: Usually by seed. Can also be grown from cuttings.

Maintenance: High.

Pollination: Male and female flowers must be present. See "Pollination," on page 65.

Suitability for Containers: Excellent. Ideal for greenhouses.

Landscape Quality: Excellent.

Nurseries: E, I, O, P, Q, S, U, Y.

Information: 1, 2, 14.

may weigh up to 10 pounds and be more than 15 inches long. The flesh may be yellow, orange, or pink. The flavor is less intense than that of the Hawaiian papaya but is still delicious and extremely enjoyable. They are also slightly easier to grow than Hawaiian papayas.

Babacos are long, seedless fruit with yellow, melon-flavored flesh. They need warm winters and part shade in areas with hot summers. Babacos are ideally suited to container culture.

Papayas grow quickly and begin producing fruit within a year of germination. Because the fruit quality declines as the plants age, however, they should be replaced every three to four years.

Adaptation

Papayas have exacting climate requirements for vigorous growth and fruit production. They must have warmth throughout the year and will be damaged by light frosts. Cold, wet soil is almost always lethal. Cool temperatures will alter fruit flavor. Thus, for most of the country, papayas are limited to greenhouses.

Pollination

Papayas have an interesting flowering habit. Plants may produce only female flowers, only male flowers, or both. To complicate matters, the plants may change from one form to another during their life cycle. In any case, male and female flowers must be present to produce fruit, so plant at least three or four plants in a group to ensure pollination. The illustrations on this page will help you identify which type of flowers you have.

Certain varieties have a propensity for producing certain types of flowers. For example, 'Solo' seedlings have flowers of both sexes 66 percent of the time, so two out of three plants will produce fruit, even if planted singly.

Propagation

Most papayas are grown from seed. To start a papaya plant, extract the seeds from ripe papayas, wash them to remove the gelatinous covering, and plant them at once. The reason for immediate planting is that the seeds lose their viability rapidly in storage. Plant the seeds in warm (80° F), sterile potting mix. They will germinate in 10 to 15 days. Seedling papayas do not

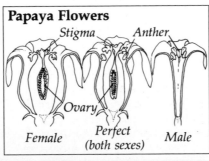

Papaya Flowers

Stigma *Anther*

Ovary

Female *Perfect (both sexes)* *Male*

transplant well. Plant in large containers so the seedlings will have to be transplanted only once—when they go into the ground. Transplant carefully, making sure not to damage the rootball.

To prevent damping off, drench the potting mix with a fungicide containing benomyl or captan.

Papayas can be propagated from semihardwood cuttings, but this is difficult and rarely done for types that grow well from seed.

Site Selection and Planting

Choose a planting site with an eye toward maximizing heat and sun. If possible, plant your papayas along a south-facing wall. Papayas also require well-drained soil; the smallest amount of excess moisture can kill them. Many gardeners go to great lengths to provide excellent drainage, such as installing drain tiles and planting on beds of perlite. Papayas do not tolerate salty water or soil.

Plant papayas carefully without breaking the rootball. Set the plants a little high to allow for settling. Use a mulch, but keep it away from the trunk. A plastic mulch will help keep soil warm and dry in wet winter areas, but remove it as soon as the weather becomes warm.

Caring for Papaya Plants

Watering   Watering is the most critical aspect in raising papayas. The plants should be kept on the dry side to avoid root rot, but also need enough water to support their large leaves.

Fertilizing   Papayas require regular applications of nitrogen fertilizers but the exact rates have not been established. Feed monthly and adjust the rate according to the plants' response.

Pruning   Papayas do not need to be pruned, but some growers pinch the seedlings or cut back established plants to encourage multiple trunks. To ensure cross-pollination and high-quality fruit, however, plant three or four separate plants and replace them every four years. Seedlings usually begin flowering 9 to 12 months after they germinate.

Pests and Diseases   Fruit flies can ruin fruit in Hawaii and Florida. Consult local university exten-

Papayas often surprise with their unusual fruit arrangement.

sion agents for control measures. Thrips, mites, and whiteflies are potential problems in some areas, as are powdery mildew, anthracnose, and various virus diseases. Avoid root rot and nematodes by planting in well-drained soils.

Harvest and Storage

Harvest papayas when most of the skin is yellow-green. After several days of ripening at room temperature, they should be almost fully yellow and slightly soft to the touch. Dark green fruit will not ripen properly off the tree, even though it may turn yellow on the outside, nor will it contain viable seed. Fully mature fruit will have edible dark brown-to-black seeds, the size of small peas, completely filling the internal cavity. The seeds have a spicy flavor that complements many sauces and salad dressings. Mature fruit can be stored at 45° F for about three weeks.

Papayas at the Table

When combined with mangoes, peaches, Indian spices, citrus, sugar, and vinegar, papayas make a chutney that enhances a myriad of dishes, whether they be Indian curries or kabobs or French-style pork or game. But the papaya is so beautiful, sweet, and fragrant that creative cooks also make use of it in simple dishes that don't require cooking.

Papayas are incredibly versatile. Here are just a few ideas: papaya served with raw-cured ham; papaya pared, sliced, and spread into a fan, served with a few of its pretty, bitter seeds on a bed of watercress with a wedge of lime; papaya sliced and pared with smoked duck, toasted walnuts, and a walnut oil vinaigrette; papaya halves filled with aioli (homemade mayonnaise with crushed garlic), shredded chicken, and cilantro; papaya chunks and scallops tossed with Greek lemon sauce; papaya puréed in a food mill, mixed with a little lime juice, and poured over ice cream; papaya chunks with candied ginger bits and sugar wafers; papaya mousse; and papaya pie.

Papayas contain an enzyme called papain ("pa-pa-yin") which, when extracted from the fruit, is sold as a meat tenderizer.

Papayas are also rich in vitamins A and C, and some say they aid digestion.

Passion Fruit

The passion fruit is a member of a large family of vining plants, many of which are grown as ornamentals for their beautiful flowers and delicate leaves. Several species and varieties produce edible fruit, but the most widely available is the purple granadilla, *Passiflora edulis*. The purple granadilla is discussed in the paragraphs that follow; other species and varieties are described in the chart on page 67.

The passion vine (and its fruit) was named by Spanish missionaries to whom its intricate and strikingly beautiful flowers represented the passion of Christ. The blooms are 2 to 3 inches in diameter, have five white sepals with green outsides, five white petals, and a corona of hairlike filaments, purple at the base and white above. The stamens are united to form a tube that supports the ovary and three prominent styles. The ten petals and sepals were thought to represent the ten Apostles present at the Crucifixion, Peter and Judas being absent. The corona of filaments represents a crown of thorns or possibly a halo. The stamens represent the five wounds and the styles symbolize the hammers used to drive the three nails.

The fruit are egg-shaped, 1½ to 2 inches in diameter, and dark purple when ripe. The rind is inedible. The orange pulp surrounds small black seeds, which are usually

Common Name: Passion fruit, granadilla.

Botanical Name: *Passiflora* species.

Origin: Tropical America.

Growth Habit: Vigorous, climbing evergreen vine that clings by tendrils. Can grow 15 to 20 feet per year once established. Must have strong support. Generally short-lived (5 to 7 years).

Adaptation: Prefers a frost-free climate. Won't take high heat.

Harvest Season: Within 60 to 80 days after bloom.

Begins Bearing: Within 2 to 3 years from seed.

Propagation: Most commonly from seed. Disease-free plants can be propagated by cuttings. Some varieties grafted.

Maintenance: High.

Pollination: Purple passion fruit is self-fruitful, but pollination is best under humid conditions. Some other varieties may require cross-pollination.

Suitability for Containers: Excellent. Good indoors.

Landscape Quality: Excellent. Often grown as an ornamental.

Nurseries: A, I, O, P, Q, R, S, U, Y.

Information: 1, 2, 8, 13, 14.

Passiflora alata. The leaves, flowers, and fruit of the passion vine are all ornamental.

strained from the pulp prior to its use as a juice or flavoring.

The passion vine has delicate, three-lobed leaves with serrated edges and a glossy, light green sheen. It grows extremely fast and requires heavy pruning to keep it in bounds. The tendrils of the vine cling to almost any support.

Adaptation

Passion fruit grows best in frost-free climates, although the vines may survive for very short periods at temperatures below freezing. The vines may lose some of their leaves in cool winters. The roots may resprout if the top is killed. The passion vine does not grow well in intense summer heat.

Propagation

Fresh seeds from superior fruit usually produce vines with good fruit. Seeds germinate in 10 to 20 days and should not be exposed to light during germination. Seed stored for more than 8 to 12 months loses viability quickly.

Nematode and soil disease problems of the purple granadilla have led to the use of the more resistant yellow passion fruit (*Passiflora edulis flavicarpa*) as a rootstock. The plants are tip-grafted when each is about ¼ inch in diameter. After grafting wrap the graft in plastic to keep it moist, and keep the plant in low light. Place the plant outdoors, leaving it there for a longer period each day, after the graft has taken.

Semihardwood cuttings will root easily under mist. Be sure to propagate only disease-free plants.

Site Selection and Planting

Excellent drainage is absolutely necessary. Also, the soil should be rich in organic matter and low in salts. Because the vines are shallow-rooted, they will benefit from a thick layer of organic mulch. Plant in full sun except in very hot areas, where partial shade is preferable.

Plant the vines next to a chain link fence or install a strong trellis before planting.

Caring for Passion Vines

Watering   Plants must have consistent moisture, or harvest and fruit quality will be reduced.

Fertilizing   These vigorous plants require regular applications of balanced fertilizer. Too much nitrogen, however, results in vigorous foliage growth at the expense of flowers.

Pruning   Pruning is necessary to keep the vines within bounds and to make harvesting easy. In warm winter climates, prune immediately after harvest. In areas with cool winters, prune in early spring.

Fruiting occurs in the leaf axils of the current season's growth, so regular pruning to maintain vigorous growth from main branches will keep the plants productive. As a general rule, remove all weak growth and cut back vigorous growth by at least one third. Left unpruned, passion vines will grow out of control and produce fruit well out of reach. However, in very hot climates, allow a thick canopy of foliage to grow around the fruit to prevent sunburn.

Pests and Diseases   Snails can be a serious problem in California. They can completely strip a vine of leaves and bark, killing young plants or predisposing them to disease. Passion vines are also susceptible to nematodes and viruses as well as the diseases that thrive in cool soils, such as fusarium.

Harvest and Storage

The fruit will quickly turn from green to deep purple when ripe and then fall to the ground within a few days. They can either be picked when they change color or gathered from the ground each day.

To store passion fruit, wash and dry them gently and place them in polyethylene bags. They should last two to three weeks at 50° F. Even slightly shriveled fruit can still be eaten. Both the fruit and the juice freeze well.

Passion Fruit Species

SPECIES	FRUIT DESCRIPTION	FLOWER DESCRIPTION	COMMENTS
Passiflora alata Fragrant granadilla	Oval, 3 to 5 inches long, yellow skin with white pulp. Aromatic.	Large and fragrant. Red, green, and white.	Oval, unlobed leaves. Winged stems. Self-pollinating.
Passiflora coccinea Red granadilla	Oval, 2 inches, skin is yellowish orange with green stripes. Sweet, white pulp.	Scarlet to orange, pink, white, and purple.	Serrated leaves, no lobes. Fruit hard and brittle at maturity. Requires cross-pollination.
Passiflora edulis Purple granadilla	Oval, 2 inches, skin is purple, pulp yellow, seeds black. Highly aromatic, good quality.	Large. White and purple.	Flowers open in morning, close by noon. Leaves attractive, lobed, and deeply toothed. Best in cooler climates. Self-pollinating.
Passiflora edulis flavicarpa Yellow passion fruit	Round to oval, 2 to 3½ inches, skin yellow, flesh dark orange, seeds brown. Fair quality.	Large. White and purple.	Flowers open at noon during spring, summer, and fall. May require cross-pollination.
Passiflora incarnata Maypop	Oval, 2 inches, yellow skin. Tart, apricot flavor.	White, lavender, and pinkish purple.	Deeply lobed, toothed leaves. Native to the eastern United States. Freezes to the ground in winter.
Passiflora laurifolia Yellow granadilla	Oval, 2 to 3½ inches, skin lemon yellow to orange, pulp white. Pear flavor.	Purple, blue, and rose.	Produces few flowers. Undivided leaves. Requires cross-pollination.
Passiflora ligularis Sweet granadilla	Oval, 2½ to 4 inches, skin is purplish yellow, pulp white. Sweet, distinctive flavor.	Greenish white.	Best in cool climates.
Passiflora maliformis Sweet calabash	Globe shaped, 1½ inches, skin is yellowish green, pulp white. Grape flavor.	Long, narrow, undivided leaves. Self-pollinating.	
Passiflora mollissima Banana passion fruit	Oval, 2½ inches. Skin is yellowish, flesh white.	White, pink, and purple.	Best in a cool climate. Prized for making juice. Lobed, serrated leaves.
Passiflora quadrangularis Giant granadilla	Oblong, 8 to 12 inches, skin is yellowish green with pink tint.	Reddish purple and white.	Large fruit weighs up to 1 pound. Whiteish rind eaten like watermelon. Oval, unlobed leaves.

Passion Fruit at the Table

You can cut passion fruit in half and scoop out the meat with a spoon in order to eat it out-of-hand, make jelly, or, with the help of a juicer and the addition of a little sugar, make passion fruit juice. The juice can also be used in ice cream, sorbet, or mousse.

Oriental Persimmon

The Oriental persimmon may seem a bit out of place in a book on subtropical fruit. It's the hardiest fruit described and can be grown outdoors in more areas than any other plant in this book. But it also has much in common with other fruit discussed here. Probably most important is that it is a fruit that is unappreciated and unfamilar to many people. It's rarely seen in supermarkets, and most people wouldn't know how to eat one if it were. Like many of the fruits decribed in this book, persimmons deserve a more important place in the American diet.

The Oriental persimmon is an extremely handsome tree that lights up the landscape in the fall when its glossy, deep green leaves turn brilliant shades of yellow, orange, and red. When the leaves drop they reveal the bright orange fruit dangling among the bare branches. The fruit ranges from the size of a baseball to that of a small grapefruit. They can be round, heart shaped, flattened, or ridged.

Varieties of Oriental persimmons are divided into two types: astringent and nonastringent. Astringent persimmons are inedible when hard and must be allowed to soften before they develop their full sweetness and flavor. Nonastringent varieties can be eaten when hard, as soon as they develop their characteristic color.

Adaptation

The Oriental persimmon does best in areas that have moderate winters and relatively mild summers. It can tolerate temperatures of 0° F when fully dormant, but because of its low chilling requirement (less than 100 hours) may break dormancy during early warm spells only to be damaged by spring frosts later. Trees generally do not produce well in the high summer heat of desert regions.

Pollination

Most of the varieties described here will set seedless fruit without being pollinated; when pollination does occur, the fruit will have seeds. Most named varieties produce only female flowers. When male flowers are present, the fruit is seedy. Most gardeners prefer seedless fruit, but some insist that persimmons develop peak flavor only when the fruit results from pollination.

Propagation

Budding or grafting your own trees allows you to take special care of the seedling rootstock. Many nursery-grown trees have had their taproot cut. Such plants are less drought resistant and should be thinned when planted.

Eastern nurseries often graft Oriental persimmons onto American persimmon (*Diospyros virginiana*) rootstocks because of the native species's extra hardiness. This is not recommended in the southern United States where the American species has been ravaged by persimmon wilt.

Consult your local extension agent for more information.

Site Selection and Planting

Full sun and well-drained soil with a pH range of 5.0 to 6.5 is ideal, but persimmons are fairly adaptable trees that can withstand a wide range of conditions as long as the soil is not overly salty.

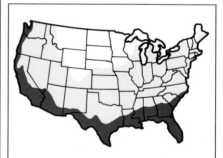

Common Name: Oriental persimmon, Japanese persimmon.

Botanical Name: *Diospyros kaki*.

Origin: Asia. Most varieties developed in Japan or China.

Growth Habit: Multitrunked or single-stemmed deciduous tree to 25 feet high and at least as wide.

Adaptation: Widely adapted to areas where winter temperatures do not drop below 0° F. Very low chilling requirement.

Harvest Season: Fall to early winter.

Begins Bearing: In 4 to 5 years.

Propagation: Can be grown from seed, but grafting or budding of named varieties is most common.

Maintenance: Low.

Pollination: Most varieties are self-fruitful.

Suitability for Containers: Suitable only for very large containers.

Landscape Quality: Excellent.

Nurseries: B, D, F, G, H, I, J, K, L, N, O, T.

Information: 1, 2, 3, 5, 8, 9, 11, 12, 13, 14.

The weeping habit of the persimmon is accentuated by a load of fruit.

Persimmons have a strong taproot, which will, hopefully, be intact when you are planting. This may mean you will have to dig a deeper hole than usual in order to plant the tree. Trees are usually available bare root or in containers.

Caring for Persimmon Trees

Watering   Persimmon trees will withstand short periods of drought, but the fruit will be larger and of higher quality with regular watering. Extreme drought will cause the leaves and fruit to drop prematurely. Any fruit left on the tree will probably sunburn.

Fertilizing   Most trees do well with a minimum of fertilizing. Excess nitrogen can cause fruit drop. If leaves are not deep green and shoot growth is less than a foot per year, apply a balanced fertilizer such as 10-10-10 at a rate of 1 pound per inch of trunk diameter at ground level. Spread the fertilizer evenly under the canopy in late winter or early spring.

Pruning   Prune to develop a strong framework of main branches while the tree is young. Otherwise the fruit, which is borne at the tips of the branches, may be too heavy and cause breakage. Mature Oriental persimmons require very little pruning other than the removal of broken or crisscrossing branches and suckers. Occasional thinning will reduce the load on the branches.

Even though the trees grow well on their own, persimmons can be pruned heavily as a hedge, as a screen, or to control size. They even make a nice espalier.

Pests and Diseases   Persimmons are relatively problem-free.

Harvest and Storage

Harvest astringent varieties when they are still hard but fully colored. They will soften on the tree and improve in quality, but you will probably lose many fruit to the birds. Astringent persimmons will ripen off the tree if stored at room temperature. They are ready to eat when they soften to a texture like that of pudding.

Nonastringent persimmons are ready to harvest when they are fully colored, but for best flavor, allow them to soften slightly before harvest.

Both kinds of persimmons should be cut from the tree with hand-held pruning shears, leaving the calyx (the leaflike collar) and a small piece of stem attached to the fruit. Even though the fruit is relatively hard when harvested, it will bruise easily, so handle with care.

Mature, hard astringent persimmons can be stored in the refrigerator for at least a month. They can also be frozen for six to eight months. They will be soft and ready to eat when thawed.

Nonastringent persimmons deteriorate quickly in the refrigerator, but they can be stored for a short period at room temperature.

Oriental Persimmon Relatives

The American persimmon, *Diospyros virginiana*, is a hardy tree native to the United States, and can be found from Connecticut south to Florida and west to Texas and Kansas. It can withstand temperatures as low as -20° F but also has a low chilling requirement, making it a good choice for the Southeast and for Southern California. The tree is similar to the Oriental persimmon, but is slightly larger. The fruit is smaller and astringent, so it must be allowed to soften completely before it can be eaten. Planting two trees ensures pollination and heavy yields.

American persimmons can be grown from seed, but the fruit quality is unpredictable. Selected

Oriental Persimmon Varieties

VARIETY	FRUIT DESCRIPTION	COMMENTS
Chocolate	Small, skin reddish orange, flesh brown-streaked when cross-pollinated. Astringent.	Named for flesh color. Vigorous, upright tree.
Eureka	Medium, bright red, flattened. Very productive. Astringent.	One of the best for southern gardeners. Bears early. Vigorous, small, dense tree.
Fuyu (Fuyugaki)	Medium, orangish red, slightly flattened. Nonastringent.	Tree vigorous, spreading. New growth has yellow tinge. 'Giant Fuyu' resembles 'Fuyu', but bears inferior fruit.
Hachiya	Large, yellow-orange, heart-shaped. Astringent.	One of the most common. Upright and slightly spreading.
Tanenashi	Medium, yellowish orange, cone-shaped. Ripens early. Astringent.	Vigorous, rounded tree. Common in Florida.

Persimmon fruit decorate the tree after the leaves have fallen.

Astringent persimmons are sweet and flavorful only after they become soft.

American persimmon: Diospyros virginiana

varieties are sometimes hard to find, but are worth seeking out. 'Meader' is almost seedless and very hardy. 'Early Golden' and 'Griffith 11' ripen in mid-September. 'John Rick' ripens about a month later. Other selections include 'Woobright', 'Miller', 'Killen', and 'Ennis Seedless'.

The black sapote, *Diospyros digyna*, is a tender evergreen shrub or small tree that can be killed by the slightest frost. The fruit weighs from 3 to 8 ounces and has the shape of a 'Fuyu' persimmon. The fruit remains dark olive green when mature. The pulp is soft, dark, and chocolate brown—hence the name "black sapote." It is non-astringent and sweet, with a texture similar to an Oriental persimmon. The trees are usually grown from seed, but some superior selections are available.

Persimmons at the Table

Soft, astringent fruit are delicious and attractive simply halved and eaten with a spoon. They are also a common ingredient in puddings, pies, and quick breads. Nonastringent varieties, which can be eaten hard, are appropriate for salads, as an accompaniment to cured or game meats, or as a garnish. They are also quite enjoyable quartered and eaten plain.

Persimmon Cake

- ½ cup butter or margarine
- 1 cup sugar
- 3 eggs, beaten
- 1 teaspoon vanilla extract
- 2 cups flour
- 1 teaspoon baking soda
- 1 teaspoon ground cinnamon
- 1 teaspoon ground nutmeg
- 1 teaspoon ground cloves
- 1 cup buttermilk
- 1½ cups persimmon pulp
- ½ cup shredded coconut
- ½ cup chopped nuts

1. Preheat oven to 350° F. In large bowl of electric mixer, cream together butter and sugar. Beat in eggs and vanilla. Sift together flour, baking soda, cinnamon, nutmeg, and cloves, and add to creamed mixture a little at a time, alternating with buttermilk. Stir in persimmon pulp, coconut, and nuts.

2. Grease and flour a 10-inch tube pan; spoon batter into prepared pan. Bake until a skewer inserted into center of cake comes out clean, about 1 hour.
Serves 8 to 10.

Tree Tomato

The tree tomato is a member of the *Solanaceae* family, which includes many useful edible plants, such as eggplants, tomatoes, and potatoes. As you would expect, this family of plants is receiving considerable attention from breeders who hope to develop new types of edible fruit and vegetables. Another interesting fruiting member of the *Solanaceae*, the pepino, is decribed at right under "Tree Tomato Relatives."

The fruit of the tree tomato faintly resembles its close relative, the common garden tomato. Both red-fruited and yellow-fruited types are available. They are generally egg-shaped and range from 1½ to 3 inches in diameter. A thin skin covers an orange flesh containing edible seeds. The flavor is sweet-tart, with yellow types usually being a little sweeter. Most people sweeten the fruit before eating.

The tree tomato produces large, oblong leaves that may reach 10 inches long. It is partially deciduous in cold climates. Small, pink flowers are usually borne in late summer and fall, but may appear at almost any time. Tree tomatoes have been grown as houseplants for years.

Adaptation

The foliage of the tree tomato is damaged in a light frost, but the

Common Name: Tree tomato, tamarillo.
Botanical Name: *Cyphomandra betacea*.
Origin: Peruvian Andes.
Growth Habit: Fast-growing evergreen or partially deciduous shrub or small tree. Has an upright form 10 to 12 feet tall.
Adaptation: Frost-free climates.
Harvest Season: Varies, but usually winter.
Begins Bearing: Within 2 to 3 years from seed.
Propagation: Usually grown from seed, but can also be propagated by cuttings under mist.
Maintenance: Low.
Pollination: Self-fruitful.
Suitability for Containers: Well suited.
Landscape Quality: Good.
Nurseries: E, I, O, Y.
Information: 1, 2, 13, 14.

plant will usually survive temperatures several degrees below freezing. Otherwise, tree tomatoes are adaptable to a variety of climates.

Site Selection and Planting

Tree tomatoes grow best in full sun except in hot, dry climates, where partial shade is better. They prefer

Tree tomato: Cyphomandra betacea

a well-drained soil that is rich in organic matter. Protect the plants from strong winds.

Caring for Tree Tomatoes
Water and fertilize regularly to keep the plants healthy and growing vigorously.

Pinch the plants when they are young to encourage branching, and prune them as they mature to keep them from growing too tall.

Aphids and nematodes are potential problems.

Harvest and Storage
Tree tomatoes are ready to harvest when they develop the yellow or red color characteristic of the particular variety. Harvesting is easy—simply pull the fruit from the tree with a snapping motion, leaving the 1- to 2-inch stem attached. You can store the fruit in the refrigerator for up to 10 weeks, but temperatures below 38° F can cause the skin to discolor.

Tree Tomato Relatives
The pepino (*Solanum muricatum*) is also known as the melon shrub, melon pear or pear-melon. These names hint at the fruit's flavor: a combination of cantaloupe and honeydew melon. It is most often eaten fresh. The oblong fruit are usually 2 to 4 inches long, but may grow to 6 inches. The skin is purplish green when ripe and the flesh ranges from light greenish yellow to a darker yellow-orange.

The pepino is an upright, spreading plant that grows 2 to 3 feet high with silky green leaves. The small, bright blue flowers will not set fruit unless the night temperatures are above 65° F. The fruit matures 30 to 80 days after pollination. The plant may need to be staked like a tomato plant.

Pepino varieties include 'Toma', 'Corazona Oro', 'Vista', 'Rio Bamba', and 'Misiki Prolific'.

Tree Tomatoes at the Table
Tree tomatoes can be served fresh, cut in half and eaten with a spoon, but most people prefer to sweeten them a little. Skin the fruit as you would a tomato by dipping it in boiling water for 20 to 30 seconds. The skin will then peel off easily.

One easy method of serving is to slice the peeled fruit, sprinkle it with sugar to taste, and chill it overnight. The fruit also makes a good sauce for topping cheesecake, ice cream, or cake. A splash of sherry lends extra character.

White Sapote
The white sapote is a distinctive, large tree with glossy, bright green, hand-shaped leaves. It produces an abundance of round yellow fruit, 3 to 4 inches in diameter. The flesh has a smooth texture and delicious flavor reminiscent of peach or banana, and contains 3 to 5 large seeds. Green-skinned varieties have white flesh. Yellow-skinned varieties have yellow flesh.

Mature white sapotes produce such a huge crop that it is almost impossible for one family to pick it,

Common Name: White sapote, Mexican apple, zapote blanco.
Botanical Name: *Casimiroa edulis*.
Origin: Mexico and Central America.
Growth Habit: Upright, fast-growing evergreen tree reaching 25 to 50 feet high and 25 to 30 feet wide. Partially deciduous in some areas.
Adaptation: Best adapted to relatively frost-free climates, but mature trees will withstand brief periods of temperatures as low as 24° F.
Harvest Season: August through November in California. May to June or later in Florida.
Begins Bearing: Grafted plants bear in 3 to 4 years. Seedlings take 5 to 8 years.
Propagation: Seeds germinate easily, but for quality fruit, choose budded or grafted varities.
Maintenance: Moderate.
Pollination: Selected varieties are self-fruitful.
Suitability for Containers: For a short period or in a large box.
Landscape Quality: Good.
Nurseries: E, I, O, P, S, U, Y.
Information: 1, 2, 13, 14.

let alone consume it. Unpicked fruit can be a problem because it drops from the tree as it ripens, making a mess and attracting bees and other insects.

Adaptation
Although the trees are hardy to 24° F, blooming occurs during late winter and frosts may destroy flowers and young fruit. Young trees can be damaged at 30° F. White sapotes do poorly in areas with high summer heat, such as the deserts of the Southwest, and in the high humidity of the tropical lowlands of Florida and Hawaii. They are well adapted to southern and central Florida and Southern California.

Propagation
Fresh seed will usually germinate in 3 to 4 weeks at 70° to 80° F. When the rootstock is ⅜ inch in diameter, it can be side- or veneer-grafted, or shield- or T-budded. Spring is the best time for grafting outdoors, but it can be done anytime in a greenhouse.

Site Selection and Planting
White sapote prefers a well-drained soil with a pH between 5.5 and 7.5, but the trees will grow in almost any soil as long as it is well-drained and the trees are not overwatered.

Before planting, consider the mess made by unpicked fruit: Planting over a patio could be a big mistake. Fallen fruit can be raked from a lawn, but this is still a chore.

White sapote: Casimiroa edulis *'Blumenthal'*

Caring for Sapote Trees

Watering   White sapote trees are drought tolerant but produce better fruit with regular, deep watering. Deep watering is also necessary to keep greedy roots where they belong—deep. Shallow watering can encourage surface roots that will break pavement or ruin lawns. If you plant in a lawn area, mulch the area under the tree and water deeply.

Fertilizing   Sapotes require regular applications of nitrogen fertilizer to maintain healthy growth. In years when trees carry a heavy crop, apply a little extra nitrogen to help offset alternate bearing.

Pruning   Young trees tend to grow vertically, without much branching. Thus, after planting, pinch out the terminal bud to encourage branching. As the tree matures, prune it to encourage compact growth and to control size.

Pests and Diseases   The white sapote has few pest or disease problems.

Harvest and Storage

Like avocados, white sapotes should be picked when still hard and allowed to ripen at room temperature. The green-skinned fruit undergoes a very subtle color change as they reach maturity, and it is difficult to tell when they are fully ripe. This is one reason why people prefer the yellow-skinned varieties, which develop a yellowish cast when they are ready to pick. Fruit will soften if picked too soon, but the flavor will be astringent. Mature fruit can be stored for brief periods only, but mashed pulp can be frozen and stored for 8 to 12 months.

Most varieties of white sapote ripen over a period of several weeks. Some, however, such as 'Suebelle', ripen over a much longer period, up to 6 months. This is an advantage if you cannot use a lot of fruit all at once.

Sapotes at the Table

The best way to enjoy sapotes is to eat them fresh with a spoon, but the pulp can also be mashed and made into an interesting sauce with a little lime or lemon juice.

Sapotes are also delicious in baked goods such as White Sapote Crumb Squares.

White Sapote Crumb Squares

- 1   cup flour
- 1   cup brown sugar, packed
- ½   cup butter or margarine, softened
- 1   teaspoon ground cinnamon
- 3   cups sapote pulp

1. Preheat oven to 350° F. In a bowl mix flour, brown sugar, butter and cinnamon until crumbly.

2. Oil an 8-inch baking dish. Arrange half the fruit in bottom, and spread half of crumb mixture on top. Layer in remaining fruit, and top with the remaining crumb mixture. Bake 40 minutes.

Makes 1 dozen squares.

White sapote trees bear their crop over a long period in summer.

White Sapote Varieties

VARIETY	FRUIT DESCRIPTION	COMMENTS*
Blumenthal	Medium, greenish yellow. Ripens September to November.	Recommended for southern Florida. Must be cross-pollinated; plant with Dade.
Chapman	Medium to large, round, slightly ribbed, yellowish green. White flesh. Ripens September to January.	Very good quality.
Chestnut	Medium to large, round, skin green, flesh golden. Ripens August to September.	Large, tall tree. Tends to bear heavily in alternate years. Good-quality fruit.
Cuccio	Medium, green. Ripens October to November.	Precocious tree; often bears second year after planting. Heavy producer.
Dade	Medium, yellowish green. Ripens September to October.	Excellent quality. Recommended for southern Florida. Must be cross-pollinated; plant with Blumenthal. Skin not bitter.
Denzler	Small, yellow. Ripens October to December.	Recommended for Hawaii. Bears lightly. Good dooryard tree.
Ecke	Small, bright yellow. Ripens October to November.	Skin becomes colored several weeks before ripening.
Fiesta	Small, thick, green. Ripens September to December.	Dependable production.
Lemon Gold	Medium, round, smooth, light yellow. Ripens October to November.	Dependably produces attractive, high-quality fruit. Fruit keeps well, resists bruising.
Louise	Small to medium, yellow. Ripens January to September.	Ripens nearly the year around in frost-free areas. Bears heavy crops of high-quality fruit.
McDill	Medium to large, round, yellowish green. Ripens November to December.	Excellent quality. Vigorous tree bears early.
Michele	Small, light yellow, slight caramel flavor. Ripens April to November.	Small tree bears light, good-quality crop.
Pike	Large, pointed, dark green. Thin, bitter skin. Ripens September to December.	Small, dependable tree.
Suebelle	Small to medium, light golden yellow. Ripens July to April.	Nearly everbearing in frost-free areas. Bears light, good-quality crop.
Sunrise	Small, green to golden. Ripens October to November.	Tall tree dependably produces fruit of excellent quality.
Vernon	Medium to large, round, yellowish green. Ripens November to January.	Does well in coastal areas. Dependable producer.
Vista	Small, oblong, light yellow. Ripens October to November.	Tends to bear in alternate years.

Unless otherwise noted, these varieties are best adapted to California.

Other Subtropical Fruits

A tremendous number of plants will produce edible fruit in subtropical climates. The better ones that were not covered in the previous chapters are listed alphabetically by botanical name in the charts below and on the following two pages. They range in cold tolerance from the hardy pawpaw, to the sensitive acerola cherry. Some species, such as the pineapple, can be grown as houseplants throughout the United States.

Pineapple: Ananas comosus

Coffee: Coffea arabica

Other Subtropical Fruit Species

SPECIES	PLANT DESCRIPTION	FRUIT DESCRIPTION	COMMENTS
Ananas comosus Pineapple	Evergreen, grows to 4 feet high by 6 feet wide, with rosettes of long, swordlike leaves that have sharply toothed edges. Hardy to 28° F.	Oval, yellow with tones of brown, green, and orange. Scaly texture.	Good indoor plant where temperatures stay above 68° F. Grown from division or by rooting leafy top of fruit in moist sand or peat.
Asimina triloba Pawpaw	Deciduous, shrublike plant 15 to 25 feet high by 10 to 15 feet wide. Purple flowers. Hardy to −25° F.	Yellowish brown, 5 to 7 inches long, shaped like a short, fat banana. Sweet flesh, large seeds.	Good for cold climates. Fruit falls to the ground when ripe. Select grafted plants or grow from seed.
Averrhoa carambola Star fruit	Evergreen tree grows to 25 feet high by 20 feet wide. Pink to white flower clusters. Hardy to 28° F.	Yellow to orange, 5 inches long with with 5 lengthwise ridges. Flavor ranges from very sour to sweet.	Star-shaped when sliced in cross-sections. Young trees are frost sensitive. Select grafted plants or grow from seed. Needs well-drained soil with low salt content.
Carissa macrocarpa Natal plum	Handsome, evergreen shrub, 6 to 12 feet high and 4 to 6 feet wide. Shiny green leaves. Showy, white, fragrant flowers. Thorny. Hardy to 26° F.	Round fruit is red to purple, 1 inch in diameter, with juicy red flesh.	Grow varieties selected for good fruit quality. Propagate by semihardwood cuttings. Drought tolerant.
Ceratonia siliqua Carob	Evergeen tree grows to 25 feet high by 15 to 20 feet wide. Deep green, divided leaves with rounded leaflets. Hardy to 20° F.	Grown for dark brown seed pods.	Seed pod is baked, ground, and used as chocolate substitute. Grown from seed or semihardwood cuttings. Pods may ferment on the tree in hot, humid climates. Not all trees are self-fruitful.
Clausena lansium Wampi	Evergreen shrub to 15 feet high by 10 feet wide. Handsome foliage. Small, white flowers in long clusters. Hardy to 24° F.	Yellowish, brittle shell-like skin encloses white flesh. Slightly acid flavor.	Propagated by softwood cuttings. Citrus relative.
Coffea arabica Coffee	Upright, evergreen shrub or small tree grows to 12 feet high by 4 to 6 feet wide. Small, fragrant, white flowers. Handsome, deep green leaves. Hardy to 32° F.	Smooth-skinned fruit is ¾ inch in diameter, red when ripe. Takes 7 to 9 months to ripen. Contains two seeds.	Seeds roasted to make coffee. Best in partial shade outdoors, but also a popular houseplant. Grown from seed or semihardwood cuttings.
Dovyalis caffra Kei apple	Evergreen shrub or small tree, 10 to 20 feet high by 10 feet wide. Small greenish yellow flowers. Very thorny. Hardy to 20° F.	Round fruit is 1 inch in diameter, deep yellow-orange with juicy, yellow, aromatic flesh. Tart until fully ripe.	Need male and female plants for pollination. Seedlings only 50% true to type; grow from semihardwood cuttings, or select grafted plants.

Star fruit:
Averrhoa carambola

Grumichama: Eugenia brasiliensis

Cherry of the Rio Grande: Eugenia aggregata

Longan: Euphoria longan 'Kohala'

Other Subtropical Fruit Species (continued)

SPECIES	PLANT DESCRIPTION	FRUIT DESCRIPTION	COMMENTS
Eugenia aggregata Cherry of the Rio Grande	Evergreen shrub, 10 to 15 feet high and 4 to 6 feet wide. White flowers. Peeling bark. Hardy to 20° F.	Dark red, oblong fruit, 1 inch in diameter, has a cherry flavor.	Good for making pies. Usually grown from seed.
Eugenia brasiliensis Grumichama	Attractive, small, evergreen tree, 10 to 15 feet high by 6 to 8 feet wide. Small, white flowers. Hardy to 27° F.	Purplish black fruit, ¾ inch in diameter, has sweet, white flesh.	Unreliable from seed, but easy from cuttings.
Eugenia luschnathiana Pitomba	Evergeen shrub, 10 to 15 feet high by 8 to 10 feet wide. Attractive foliage. Hardy to 27° F.	Bright yellow fruit, 1½ inches in diameter, has white flesh. Juicy, mildly acidic.	Usually grown from seed, but quality unpredictable. Makes good jam.
Eugenia uniflora Surinam cherry	Evergreen shrub or small tree, 10 to 15 feet high by 6 to 8 feet wide. Small, white flowers. Handsome foliage. Hardy to 30° F.	Dark red to black fruit, ¾ inch in diameter, with eight ribs.	Popular ornamental. Unreliable from seed, but easily grown from cuttings. Select plants with quality fruit. Good for making jellies or jams.
Euphoria longan Longan	Evergreen tree, 25 to 40 feet high and equally as wide. Upright clusters of yellowish white flowers. Hardy to 24° F.	Yellow to brown fruit, 1 inch in diameter, hang in grapelike clusters. Sweet, white flesh.	Seedlings slow to bear fruit. Propagate by air-layering. Related to litchi.
Garcinia mangostana Mangosteen	Evergreen tree, 10 to 20 feet high by 8 to 12 feet wide. Large, yellow-red flowers. Hardy to 32° F.	Dark, reddish purple fruit is round, 3 inches in diameter, with thick skin. Segmented, translucent, sweet flesh.	Yellow latex produced by all plant parts. Grow from seed or select grafted plants.
Hovenia juicina Raisin tree	Deciduous tree, 15 to 25 feet high by 8 to 12 feet wide. Small, greenish purple flowers. Hardy to −10° F.	Grown for fleshy flower stems, which taste like raisins. Small brown fruit not used.	Usually grown from seed.
Malpighia glabra Acerola cherry	Evergreen to semideciduous shrub, 6 to 10 feet high by 4 to 6 feet wide. Small, white to pink flowers. Hardy to 30° F.	Bright red, tinged yellow, cherrylike. Sweet to acid.	High in vitamin C. Fruit tends to drop in cool climates. Tomato-set hormone sprays may increase yields. Propagate by hardwood or semihardwood cuttings.
Manilkara zapota Sapodilla	Evergreen tree, 20 to 40 feet high by 15 to 30 feet wide. Small, green to brown flowers are fragrant at night. Hardy to 28° F.	Gray to brown, oval fruit, 2 to 4 inches diameter, with sweet, yellowish, translucent flesh.	Milky sap used to flavor chewing gum. Can be grown from seed, but selected varieties are preferable.

Pitomba:
Eugenia luschnathiana

Prickly pear: Opuntia ficus-indica

Tamarind: Tamarindus indica

Miracle fruit: Synsepalum dulcificum

Other Subtropical Fruit Species (continued)

SPECIES	PLANT DESCRIPTION	FRUIT DESCRIPTION	COMMENTS
Morus nigra Black mulberry	Fast-growing, deciduous tree, 20 to 25 feet high and spreading at least as wide. Hardy to 18° F.	Deep reddish purple, berrylike fruit. Very productive. Sweet.	Best pruned regularly to keep tree small and easy to harvest. Fruit stains pavement. Easy to grow from hardwood cuttings.
Myrciaria cauliflora Jaboticaba	Evergreen tree, 15 to 30 feet high by 18 to 12 feet wide. Small, white flowers produced directly on bark. Hardy to 25° F.	Reddish purple fruit is 1 inch in diameter, borne on small branches and trunk. Juicy, translucent white flesh similar to a grape.	Unusual fruiting habit. Seedlings fruit in about 8 years. Can be air-layered.
Opuntia ficus-indica Prickly pear	Evergreen, mostly thornless cactus with upright growth to 7 to 15 feet high. Attractive, yellow flowers. Hardy to 26° F.	Yellow to reddish purple fruit is oval, 3 to 4 inches in diameter, with slightly tart, red flesh.	Handle fruit carefully; skin covered with spines. Easy to propagate by rooting small padlike branches.
Pachira aquatica Malabar chestnut	Evergreen shrub to small tree, 10 to 15 feet high by 8 to 10 feet wide. Large, fragrant, greenish white to pink and red flowers. Hardy to 28° F.	Large, brown fruit contains several small, edible nuts.	Fruit splits open when ripe, seeds may fall out. Edible raw or roasted. Grown from seed.
Prunus salicifolia Capulin cherry	Evergreen to semideciduous tree, 20 to 30 feet high by 10 to 20 feet wide. Very fast growing. Shiny foliage and fragrant white flowers. Hardy to 20° F.	Cherrylike, dark purple with green flesh. Good quality.	Very low chilling requirement. Will set fruit in 3 to 4 years from seed, but quality is variable. Can be air-layered. Self-fruitful.
Saccharum officinarum Sugar cane	Upright, evergreen herb 6 to 10 feet high. Forms spreading clumps. Shoots hardy to 32° F, roots slightly hardier.	Grown for sweet, thick, green or purple canes.	Highest sugar content in midsummer to late fall. Will root at stem nodes. Can also be propagated by root division.
Synsepalum dulcificum Miracle fruit	Evergreen shrub, 6 to 10 feet high by 3 to 6 feet wide. Small, white flower clusters. Hardy to 32° F.	Red, oval fruit is ¾ inch in diameter. Succulent flesh.	Sour flavors taste sweet after eating miracle fruit. Propagate by seed, semihardwood cuttings, or air-layering.
Tamarindus indica Tamarind	Evergreen tree, 20 to 40 feet high and at least as wide. Small clusters of yellow-red flowers. Hardy to 26° F.	Grown for reddish brown, 5-inch-long pods with edible flesh surrounding small, hard seeds. Sweet-tart flavor.	Usually grown from seed. Can be grown from semihardwood and softwood cuttings. Young trees are cold sensitive.
Ziziphus jujuba Jujube	Deciduous tree, 20 to 25 feet high by 15 to 20 feet wide. Clusters of small, yellow flowers. Gnarled branches. Hardy to −20° F.	Light green to reddish brown, apple flavor.	Good for hot or cold climates. Can be eaten crisp or dried. Grow from seed or by air-layering.

Jaboticaba:
Myrciaria cauliflora

Caring for Subtropical Fruits

Subtropical fruits, like any other plants, will thrive when given proper care. In this section you'll find all you need to know about soils, fertilizers, watering, pruning, planting, propagation, and pest control.

The plants described in this book originate from all over the world and, as a group, have cultural requirements that cover the spectrum of horticultural practices. Thus it is important to consider all the requirements of a species—climate, soil, water, and pest control—before you plant.

Choosing Plants at the Nursery

Most subtropical plants are sold in the containers in which they were grown. An exception to this general practice are standard-sized citrus trees, which may be grown in field nurseries, then dug up and placed in containers (usually tall, narrow plastic containers called sleeves) for sale in nurseries. Field-grown plants have usually been pruned to compensate for roots lost during digging and do not have the full appearance that plants grown in a container have. Both types grow well once in the ground, as long as they have not been in the container too long.

When selecting container plants, look for healthy specimens that show signs of active growth. Avoid plants with signs of stagnation. These signs include yellow or poorly colored leaves, dead branches, or large, circling roots near the soil surface.

Some plants, such as persimmon

When you first plant a tree, construct a small basin a little larger than the rootball to hold water when you irrigate. As the tree grows, this basin should be enlarged.

and kiwi fruit, are sold bare-root. Bare-root plants are usually deciduous. They are dug up while dormant and sold with their roots packed in sawdust. Some mail-order nurseries also sell evergreen plants such as citrus bare-root in order to minimize shipping costs. When selecting bare-root plants, look for well-formed root systems with laterals extending in all directions. Avoid plants with damaged or dry roots. Bare-root plants must be kept cool and moist and should be planted as soon as possible.

Container plants can be planted anytime as long as they are kept moist prior to planting.

Soil Sense

For healthy growth, plants need three things from soil: moisture, nutrients, and air. Most clay soils absorb water slowly and drain poorly. As a result, these soils tend to be poorly aerated, especially after watering. If water fills too many of the air spaces for long, the roots will die, causing the top to die as

well. You know you have a clay soil if it is hard as a rock when dry and a sticky mess when wet.

Sandy soils, on the other hand, absorb water rapidly and also drain rapidly, leaving plenty of air, but little water. Also, because sandy soils don't hold nutrients well, plants growing in sandy soils need to be fertilized more frequently. You can tell you have a sandy soil if its texture is gritty.

Most soils have properties between those of sand and those of clay. These soils, called loams, vary greatly in texture and structure, but often have a desirable combination of good aeration and high water and nutrient holding capacity.

The only way to improve excessively sandy or clayey soils is to add organic matter. Peat moss, compost, and other organic materials loosen and aerate clay soils and help sandy soils hold moisture and nutrients. Sand is not a good amendment for clay soils; the particles of sand aggregate with the clay and make the soil less permeable.

How Plants Are Sold in Nurseries

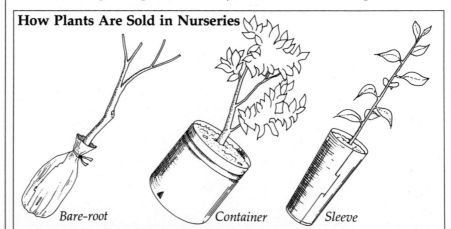

Bare-root   Container   Sleeve

Planting From Containers

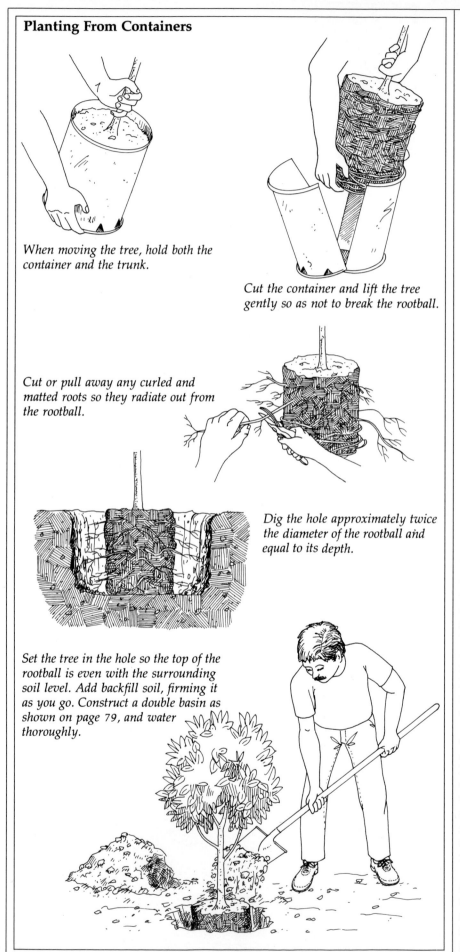

When moving the tree, hold both the container and the trunk.

Cut the container and lift the tree gently so as not to break the rootball.

Cut or pull away any curled and matted roots so they radiate out from the rootball.

Dig the hole approximately twice the diameter of the rootball and equal to its depth.

Set the tree in the hole so the top of the rootball is even with the surrounding soil level. Add backfill soil, firming it as you go. Construct a double basin as shown on page 79, and water thoroughly.

Before planting, blend 4 to 6 inches of organic matter into the top 10 to 12 inches of soil in the planting area. You may also mix organic matter with the backfill soil when planting, but avoid manure—it can burn the roots. Keep the soil under the canopy covered with mulch (see page 81). If you use an organic mulch, it will slowly decompose and continue to improve the soil.

If your soil has a hardpan or other impervious layer below the topsoil, organic matter will not improve the drainage. In such cases, it's best to plant in containers or raised beds.

Soil pH

The pH of a soil is a measure of its acidity or alkalinity. The pH scale runs from 1 (extremely acidic) to 14 (extremely alkaline). The middle of the scale (7) is the neutral point.

Soil pH is important because it affects the availability of essential nutrients. For instance, plants adapted to acidic soils often show signs of iron chlorosis when grown in alkaline soils. Most subtropical fruit grow best in slightly acid soils, but many will tolerate slightly alkaline conditions, especially if they are given foliar feedings of micronutrients.

Testing the pH of a soil is easy when you use an inexpensive kit, available at most nurseries and scientific supply houses. Most cooperative extension offices will perform soil tests or refer you to someone who can. A fee is usually charged for these tests, but they give you more data than you can get with a kit, including such helpful information as soil texture and nutrient content.

Adjusting soil pH is relatively easy. If your soil is too acidic, a common condition in areas with heavy rainfall, the most reliable cure is to add ground limestone to the soil. If alkalinity is the problem, add sulphur, aluminum sulfate, or ferrous sulfate, or fertilize with an ammonium fertilizer such as ammonium phosphate.

These soil amendments are available in most nurseries. Application rates vary according to the pH and soil type, so ask the people at your nursery or a cooperative extension agent for exact rates.

Soil Salts

Most subtropical plants are sensitive to salts. Salty soils are most commonly found in areas with low annual rainfall and alkaline soil, such as portions of the desert Southwest. These salts may originate in irrigation water or fertilizer residues. In areas that receive ample rainfall, salts are naturally leached through the root zone.

The first symptom of salt damage is slow growth. In severe cases, the edges of the leaves become burned. If you suspect that high levels of salt are damaging your plants, leach the soil by watering very deeply every third or fourth irrigation. Of course, a well-drained soil is necessary for successful leaching. If your soil is both salty and poorly drained, consider growing your subtropical plants in raised beds or containers.

Planting

The best time to plant subtropicals is in spring, after the danger of frost has passed, so the plants can become established before winter.

The illustrations on this page show how to plant container and bare-root plants.

Watering

How often you have to water and how much water you have to apply depends on a number of factors:

Soil Type   Plants grown in sandy soils need to be watered more often than those grown in clay soils.

Weather   Naturally, if you live in an area with abundant rainfall, you won't have to water as often as someone in a dry climate. It's also true that plants need more water in hot weather than in cool weather. Also, wind dries out plants more rapidly than still air does.

Type of Plant   Fast-growing, shallow-rooted plants with big leaves, such as bananas, need much more water than slow-growing, deep-rooted plants, such as persimmons. Also, because of their limited root systems, young plants need more frequent watering than established plants.

By understanding how these factors affect your specific situation, you'll be able to develop a watering schedule that suits the needs of the plants in your yard.

Water Deeply   Apply enough water to wet the entire root zone. For most citrus trees, this is at least 24 inches deep. Larger trees may need to be watered to a depth of 4 feet or more. Deep watering encourages deep rooting and extends the period the plant can go between waterings.

Soil tubes and soil augers are useful tools for determining how deeply water is penetrating and how much moisture is in the soil between irrigations. These tools are used to remove a core of soil from the root zone and examine it for moisture. In loose soils you can measure how deeply an irrigation has penetrated by pushing a stiff piece of wire or a steel rod into the soil after watering. It should move easily through the moist soil and become difficult to push when it reaches the dry soil.

Direct Water to the Roots   Use basins, furrows, or drip irrigation to direct water to the roots. If you use a basin adjust the size of the basin as the plant grows. During wet seasons make small breaks in the walls of the basin to allow excess water to drain away.

Mulches   Mulches conserve soil moisture. Spread the mulch about 4

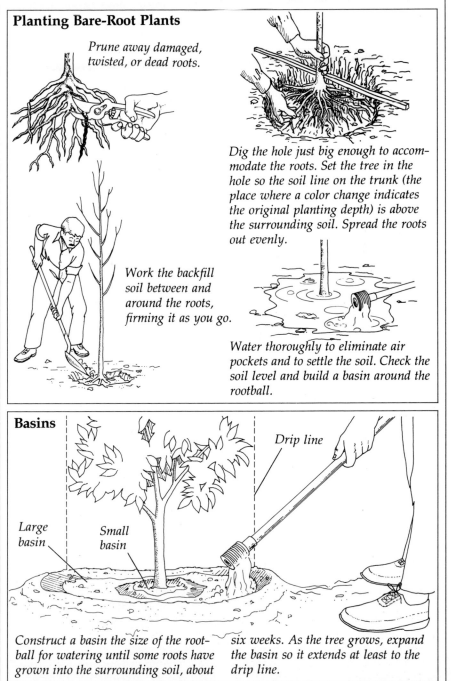

Planting Bare-Root Plants

Prune away damaged, twisted, or dead roots.

Work the backfill soil between and around the roots, firming it as you go.

Dig the hole just big enough to accommodate the roots. Set the tree in the hole so the soil line on the trunk (the place where a color change indicates the original planting depth) is above the surrounding soil. Spread the roots out evenly.

Water thoroughly to eliminate air pockets and to settle the soil. Check the soil level and build a basin around the rootball.

Basins

Drip line

Large basin

Small basin

Construct a basin the size of the root- ball for watering until some roots have grown into the surrounding soil, about   *six weeks. As the tree grows, expand the basin so it extends at least to the drip line.*

inches thick, but keep it away from the trunk. (See page 81 for more about mulches.)

How To Water
Water can be applied in several ways: in basins, by sprinklers, or by drip systems.

Basins
Soil basins simplify watering and are easy to construct. Once you know how deeply 1 inch of water will penetrate, you can adjust the height of the walls of the basin or the number of times you fill it up according to how deeply you want to irrigate. In a sandy soil 1 inch of water will usually penetrate to a depth of 12 inches. In a clay soil it may reach only 3 to 4 inches.

Sprinklers
To be effective, sprinklers must be selected carefully. The application rate of the sprinkler should match the soil's ability to absorb water. Sprinklers that apply water too fast can cause erosion and wasteful run-off. Care must be taken not to wet the tree trunks. Low-volume sprinklers, often called spitters, are usually most effective. Sprinklers have one important advantage: They can also be used for frost protection (see page 13).

Drip Systems
Drip emitters discharge water at very low rates, usually between ½ and 1 gallon per hour, to a very precise area. Evaporation and waste are kept to a minimum. A tree will need at least 4 emitters evenly distributed beneath its canopy.

Perhaps a better solution is to use a modified drip system called trickle irrigation. In this method, low volume (5 to 50 gallons per hour), low-pressure minisprinklers, which emit a fanlike spray with a radius of 3 feet or more, are substituted for emitters. The larger coverage area wets the root zone more evenly and the larger orifices of the minisprinklers are less susceptible to clogging, which is a constant problem of drip emitters.

How to Fertilize
Most fruit trees grown commercially in North America have been studied carefully to determine precisely which nutrients they need for maximum fruit quality and quantity. If you are growing peaches, apples, or cherries, your cooperative extension office can supply you with a specific fertilization program developed for your area. This is also true for several of the species in this book, including citrus, persimmons, and figs. The descriptions of these fruits in the encyclopedia section include specific information on when and how much fertilizer to apply. Unfortunately, few other subtropical fruits have been so carefully studied in North America. To fertilize these plants properly, you need to know how fertilizers affect plants. Each essential element plays a specific role in plant growth. Nitrogen stimulates leafy growth, often at the expense of flower production. It must be applied regularly, because it is quickly leached through the soil. Phosphorus and potassium tend to promote flowering and fruiting. Because they are less mobile, they don't need to be applied as frequently as nitrogen.

Overfertilization can be more damaging than underfertilization. Fertilizers are salts that leave acidic or alkaline residues; excessive use of fertilizer may burn plants and drastically alter the soil pH.

Soils and Fertilization
Soil and climate directly influence fertilization practices. Sandy soils are less fertile than clay soils, and problems caused by poor fertilization practices can develop more rapidly in sandy soils.

Soils in areas with high annual rainfall, such as Florida, are generally well leached and low in fertility. These soils are usually acidic and are deficient in many nutrients. They are generally deficient in nitrogen, phosphorus, boron, zinc, iron, manganese, copper, and molybdenum.

Soils in arid regions, such as California or Arizona, receive low annual rainfall. Little leaching has taken place, so these soils are alkaline and most essential nutrients are available in sufficient amounts. In general, nitrogen, iron, and zinc may be the only nutrients required.

A soil test is the best way to determine exactly what nutrients are available in your soil. Call your local cooperative extension office for information on soil laboratories in your area.

Reading Fertilizer Labels
Fertilizers are labeled according to how much of the three major nutrients, nitrogen (N), phosphorus (P), and potassium (K) they contain. The percentages may change, but they are always listed in this order: N, P, K. This listing, called the *analysis*, reveals two important things. Most importantly, it tells how much of a nutrient is in a fertilizer, by weight. For example, a 5-pound box of 5–10–10 fertilizer contains 5 percent nitrogen (or 0.25 pounds of *actual nitrogen*), 10 percent phosphate (a form of phosphorus), and 10 percent potash (a form of potassium). By comparing the price per pound of actual nitrogen of different fertilizers, you can determine which fertilizer is the best buy. It also helps to know the amount of nitrogen in a bag of fertilizer, because most fertilizer recommendations are given in pounds of actual nitrogen per plant or given area.

The analysis also tells the relative proportions of N, P, and K. For example, ratios of 2–1–1 (such as 10–5–5 or 20–10–10) indicate that there is twice as much nitrogen as phosphate and potash. Choose the fertilizer that contains the best proportions of N, P, and K for your growing conditions.

Types of Fertilizers
There are three basic types of fertilizers: dry, liquid, and organic.

Dry fertilizers are available in soluble and slow-release formulations. Soluble formulations are the least expensive, but they may burn the plants. Slow-release fertilizers, although expensive, are safest to use because they are less likely to burn plants.

Slow-release fertilizers are only slightly soluble in water and release nutrients to the plants over a period of time. These fertilizers remain effective in the soil for 6 weeks to 2 years, depending on the type.

The most common type of slow-release fertilizer, urea formaldehyde, is broken down by bacteria into a soluble form available to plants. Other slow-release fertilizers are coated to reduce their solubility, or formulated with slightly soluble materials that become available without bacterial activity.

The amount of slow-release nitrogen in a fertilizer is shown on the label as a part of the nitrogen analysis. It is called *water-insoluble nitrogen* and is shown as a percentage of the total fertilizer. For example, a fertilizer that is 10 percent nitrogen might contain 8 percent water-soluble nitrogen and 2 percent water-insoluble nitrogen.

Liquid fertilizers are often preferred for container plants.

Organic fertilizers are expensive, but their residues may last a long time in the soil, improving its structure. Manures contain salts which may burn the plants.

Micronutrients

Many complete fertilizers (containing N, P, and K) contain micronutrients. Sometimes, however, plants need micronutrients only. In these cases, apply a foliar spray containing chelated micronutrients in the early spring, when the new leaves are fully expanded. Chelated micronutrients are bound to a chemical that improves their absorption by the plant.

Fertilizer Rates

Here are some general guidelines for applying fertilizers.

First, it's safest to apply fertilizers three or four times during the growing season, beginning in late winter and ending in late summer. Fertilizing after late summer can delay dormancy in subtropical plants and increase the chance of damage from sudden cold weather in the fall.

Second, subtropical fruits can be categorized as light or heavy feeders. Light feeders include avocado, fig, pineapple guava, loquat, macadamia, and persimmon. They need little or no fertilizer. Banana, cherimoya, citrus, guava, kiwi fruit, litchi, mango, papaya, passion fruit, white sapote, and tree tomato are considered heavy feeders.

We recommend the following program for heavy feeders: For the first and second seasons, apply 1 to 2 tablespoons of a complete fertilizer three or four times during the growing season. Fertilizers labeled for citrus and avocados are good general purpose fertilizers for all subtropical plants. Because you are applying such small amounts, the analysis doesn't really matter at this point. From the third to the seventh or eighth year, gradually increase the feedings from ¼ pound to 1 pound actual nitrogen per year, spread out over three or four applications. From the eighth or ninth year onward, plants should receive between 1 and 1½ pounds of actual nitrogen per year.

Judging the Results

The best way to tell how much fertilizer to use is to look at the plants. Nitrogen promotes vegetative growth, and too much of it can reduce your fruit crop. Conversely, if the plants are producing only a few inches of new growth each season and the lower leaves are yellow, step up the feeding.

Mulching

Mulches are useful in many gardens, but they are particularly beneficial to subtropical plants. Mulch materials may be black plastic, ground fir bark, cocoa bean hulls, decomposed sawdust, composted grass clippings, gravel, or leaves. When properly applied, mulches improve the garden for plants and people in a variety of ways:

• They conserve soil moisture.
• They protect soil from being compacted by foot traffic.
• They reduce soil erosion.
• They moderate soil temperatures.
• They inhibit weed growth.
• If organic, they help improve the soil structure and fertility.
• Some mulches reflect extra heat into a tree to ripen fruit in cooler climates.

On the other hand, plants in mulched areas may be more susceptible to frost damage because less heat is absorbed by the soil and re-radiated at night. For best frost protection, rake the mulch away to expose the ground around the plant during cold spells, or use a gravel mulch, which, like soil, stores heat during the day and releases it at night.

Never pile any mulch against a tree trunk or plant stem, because it

Symptoms of Nutrient Deficiencies

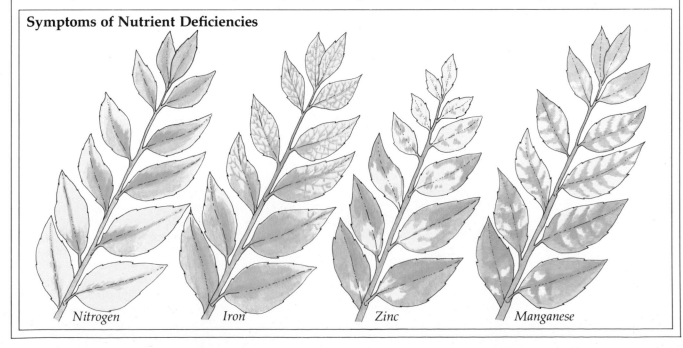

Nitrogen Iron Zinc Manganese

can cause rot. Keep it at least 6 inches away. An exception to this rule is in very cold climates, where a mulch is piled extra high to protect the trunk.

Pruning

Unlike most temperate fruit trees, which must be pruned carefully and frequently for best fruit production, most subtropical fruit species do not require drastic annual pruning. Kiwi fruit and passion fruit are two exceptions; they must be pruned regularly to promote flowering, to keep the plants under control, and to keep the fruit within easy reach.

Even though pruning may not always be necessary, in most cases you will want to prune your plants to control their size, make them more attractive, or stimulate new growth and heavier yields.

There are two types of pruning cuts: thinning and heading. Thinning cuts remove branches or limbs where they join the rest of the plant, resulting in a more open plant. By thinning main shoots back to shorter side branches, you can decrease the size of a plant without destroying its natural character.

Heading cuts remove the terminal or top of a branch, resulting in vigorous growth from dormant buds just below the cut and a denser, more compact plant. Shearing to form a hedge is a type of heading.

Both thinning and heading will control the size of a plant, but thinning usually produces a healthier, more attractive plant.

Some subtropicals, such as citrus, figs, and persimmons, can be trained as informal espaliers. An espalier is a plant trained in a flat, vertical plane, usually against a fence, wall, or trellis. Formal designs, which have a recognizable geometric pattern to the branches, are often used for apples and pears but are not practical with most subtropicals. An informal espalier often ends up looking like a hedge, although it is usually more open. Frequent pruning and tying keeps the plant flat and productive from top to bottom. Espaliers are particularly effective in areas where space is limited.

Pest and Disease Control

Most plants, when properly cared for, will resist attacks from insects and diseases. Many pesticides have been approved for use on commercially important subtropical fruits such as citrus and avocados, but other less-common fruits are rarely listed on chemical labels. In either case, the best advice for insect and disease control is to prevent problems by following good cultural practices. Drought-stressed, improperly planted, or overfertilized plants are more susceptible to pest and disease problems than vigorously growing plants.

If your plants do become infested with insects or infected by a disease, use only chemicals that are approved for use on that specific plant and follow label directions precisely. Pay particularly close attention to how close to harvest a spray can be used safely. Pest control regulations vary from state to state; if you have questions, consult your cooperative extension office.

Listed below are some of the pests and diseases that may trouble subtropical plants and recommendations for control. If a chemical control is mentioned, it does not mean it can be used on all subtropical fruit. Check the label first.

Aphids Aphids are small, soft-bodied insects that feed on plant sap. They may be yellow, green, red, purple, brown, or black, and are usually clustered on plant leaves, stems, and flowers. Some aphids are covered with a white, waxy coating.

Aphids distort the parts of the plant they feed on and, in severe infestations, stunt the whole plant. Aphids produce honeydew, a clear, shiny, sticky fluid that coats plant parts and attracts ants.

The easiest method of controlling aphids is to knock them off the plant with a hard spray of slightly soapy water. Malathion and Diazinon are also effective controls registered for use on citrus.

Caterpillars Caterpillars are larvae of moths and butterflies, and include such pests as tent caterpil-

Pruning Techniques

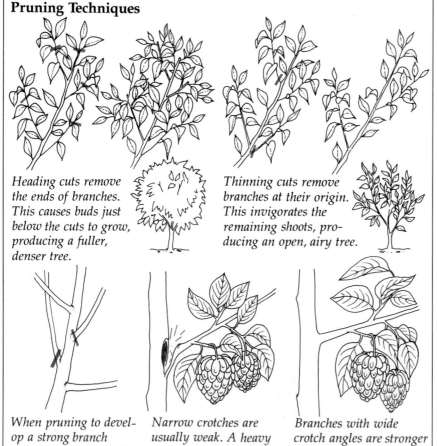

Heading cuts remove the ends of branches. This causes buds just below the cuts to grow, producing a fuller, denser tree.

Thinning cuts remove branches at their origin. This invigorates the remaining shoots, producing an open, airy tree.

When pruning to develop a strong branch structure, remove limbs with narrow crotch angles.

Narrow crotches are usually weak. A heavy crop and a little wind may cause them to break.

Branches with wide crotch angles are stronger and can support a heavier load.

lars and leaf rollers. Caterpillars may be smooth, hairy, or covered with spines. They may feed on leaves, stems, flowers, or fruit.

Diazinon is recommended for control of caterpillars on citrus. *Bacillus thuringensis*, a biological control marketed under the names Thuricide and Dipel, is an effective control for the caterpillars when they are very young.

Mealybugs Mealybugs are oval, white insects that cluster in white, cottony masses on stems and leaves. Like aphids, mealybugs suck plant juices. Infested plant parts may be distorted, yellowed, and stunted. Honeydew, a clear, shiny secretion of the mealybugs, may cover plant parts and attract ants. Malathion and Diazinon are registered for control of mealybugs on citrus and figs.

Mites Mites are tiny pests related to spiders. In fact, some mite species are commonly called spider mites. Spider mites produce webbing that covers the undersides of infested leaves and other plant parts. Their feeding causes the leaves to become stippled, discolored, and yellow. Eventually the leaves may die. Mites thrive on water-stressed, dusty plants. Thus, the best way to prevent mite problems is to water properly and occasionally spray the plants with water to keep them clean. Refined oil sprays are also effective for mite control on citrus. The miticide, dicofol (marketed under the name Kelthane), is recommended for use on citrus.

Nematodes Nematodes are microscopic worms that live in the soil and infest plant roots. They usually stunt a plant and may predispose it to infection by diseases or infestation by other pests.

In severe cases, nematodes can kill a plant. Some types of nematodes produce small nodules or bulges on the plant roots, but most of the time it's hard to tell if you have a nematode problem. Soil fumigation prior to planting is the only way to control nematodes, but usually it is easier just to live with them. If the plants are cared for properly, most will continue to be productive regardless of the nematodes. If you think nematodes are causing you serious problems, consult your local cooperative extension office.

Scale Scale look like small fish scales stuck to the plant. They may be brown, reddish, or gray, and they may be covered with a white, waxy material. Adult scales are immobile and feed on the plant's sap. Young scales have no shell and move around on the plant.

Foliage infested with scale turns yellow and may die. In severe infestations, the insects may entirely cover the trunk and branches. Like other sucking insects, scale produce honeydew, a sticky, clear, shiny material that attracts ants.

The protective shells on adult scale makes them difficult to control. On citrus, light oil sprays can be used to smother adult scale and their eggs. Malathion and Diazinon are used to control scale in its young, crawling stage.

Omnivorous looper, a pest of avocado and other plants, can be controlled with Ba-cillus thuringensis when the loopers are small.

Top: *Aphids may completely cover the new shoots of citrus. Malathion and Diazinon are recommended controls.*

Bottom: *Mealybugs may infest the leaves, stems, and fruit of citrus. Mal-athion and Diazinon are registered controls.*

Slugs and Snails   Slugs and snails feed on the flowers, young shoots, leaves, and fruit of many subtropical fruit species. They avoid direct sun and dry places, hiding during the day in damp, protected places.

Baits containing metaldehyde are recommended for use on many tropical fruit trees. You can also keep slugs and snails under control by cleaning up the debris in which they hide during the day. To reduce snail problems on citrus, prune the lower branches so they don't hang on the ground, and place a band of copper screen around the base of the trunk.

Thrips   Thrips are tiny, slender insects that infest the flowers, leaves, fruit, and shoots of many kinds of plants. They damage plants by rasping plant tissue and then sucking the released sap. Thrips distort flower petals and leaves. Damaged leaves may be flecked, streaked with yellow, and have silvery undersides dotted with shiny, black spots. Malathion and Diazinon are registered chemical controls.

Diseases
The most frequently occurring diseases of subtropical fruit are encouraged by poorly drained soil or excess water around the trunk of the plant. Trunk cankers, foot rots, and root rots can quickly kill plants and are difficult to control once they have taken hold. Watering properly, planting in well-drained soil, keeping wet soil and mulches away from trunks, and breaking basins in rainy seasons so excess water can drain away are the best preventive measures. Various fruit rots also cause problems in humid climates. Chlorothalonil is registered for control of fruit rot on papaya and passion fruit. Other controls vary depending on the area; consult your local extension specialists for appropriate control measures.

Leaf spots   Leaf spots (often referred to as anthracnose) are usually caused by fungi. In many cases they do not seriously damage the plant, but some leaf-spotting fungi will defoliate a plant, causing it to decline and eventually die. Leaf-spotting fungi are most active in mild, damp weather.

To control mild infections, simply pick off the damaged leaves. If the infection becomes serious, spray with a neutralized copper fungicide or another appropriately labeled fungicide, such as benomyl, captan, or chlorothalonil.

Fireblight   Fireblight is a bacterial disease that infects subtropical plants in the rose family, such as loquats. It is spread by contaminated splashing water, pollinating insects, and pruning shears. Fireblight symptoms are unmistakable: The tips of branches are blackened and appear to be burned (hence the name fireblight).

There are no cures for this disease, but you may reduce the severity of the infection by spraying the

Mites cause a chlorotic stippling of the leaves. Dicofol is recommended for mite control on citrus.

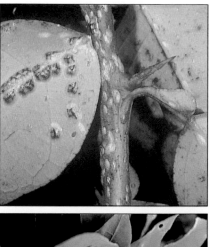

Top: *Brown soft scale on citrus. Light oil sprays will smother the scale; malathion and Diazinon will control scale in its young, crawling stage.*

Bottom: *Snails eat the leaves and new shoots of citrus and many other plants.*

plant several times while it is blooming with streptomycin or a neutralized copper spray. Stop the disease from spreading by pruning out infected branches as soon as you see them. Cut the infected branches off several inches below the blackened area. Sterilize your shears after each cut by dipping them in rubbing alcohol or a 10% solution of chlorine bleach.

Animal Pests

Birds and rodents can be as troublesome as any insect or disease.

Many bird species will feed on ripening fruit. The most effective way to deter them from devouring your harvest is to cover the plants with protective netting, available in most nurseries and garden centers.

Mice, voles, and rabbits will eat the bark of young trees. If enough bark is removed to girdle the tree, the roots will die and the shoots will wither. Protect the trunk with hardware cloth or narrow wire mesh. Check the material occasion-ally to make sure it doesn't slip or girdle the tree.

Propagating Subtropical Fruits

The more you experiment with growing subtropical fruits, the more you'll want to propagate your own plants. Nurseries will not always be the best source of the varieties you desire, so you will inevitably have to grow plants from seed or propagate a friend's plant by rooting cuttings, budding, or grafting. Grafting and budding techniques can also be used to restore the top of a tree that has been killed below the bud union or to place pollinating limbs in trees that require cross-pollination.

There are five basic methods of propagating plants: germinating seed, rooting cuttings, budding and other forms of grafting, layering, and dividing. The success of each method varies among species and even among varieties of the same species.

Anyone who becomes a serious propagator will need additional information. The best reference on this subject is *Plant Propagation, Principles and Practices* by Hudson Hartmann and Dale Kester, published by Prentice-Hall. Ortho's book *How To Build & Use Greenhouses* discusses the facilities that are often required for propagating subtropical fruit.

Growing Plants From Seed

Most subtropical fruits can be propagated from seed. Exceptions include the seedless citrus, persimmon, pineapple, and banana. Because fruit quality and other characteristics of most plants are variable in seed-grown plants, however, this propagation method is usually used only to produce rootstocks that will later be grafted or budded to selected varieties.

Papaya, passion fruit, and tamarillo are examples of fruit that can be propagated from seed. You could take seed from supermarket fruit,

Top: *Thrips rasp silvery patterns on the leaves and fruit of citrus. Malathion and Diazinon are registered for control of thrips on citrus.*

Bottom: *Fireblight infects the shoots of loquat and other plants in the rose family.*

Anthracnose caused by Cercospora *infects the leaves and forms sunken lesions on the fruit of avocados in Florida and along the Gulf Coast. Spray with basic copper sulfate.*

germinate it, and expect the resulting plant to produce good fruit. With other fruit, you never know what you'll get, and plants will probably take years to bear fruit.

Germination requirements differ for each plant, but in general, seeds need warm temperatures, moisture, and a suitable medium to germinate. Seeds from most subtropical fruits germinate best if the soil temperature is maintained between 70° and 80° F. To accomplish this, you'll need to supply bottom heat to keep the soil warm. There are many products on the market designed to heat a flat of soil.

Seeds from some deciduous fruits, including kiwi fruit, persimmon and pomegranate, require a long period of cold storage (stratification) at temperatures between 32° and 40° F before they will germinate. Such chilling simulates the natural winter conditions necessary to break dormancy. To stratify seeds, place them in a plastic bag filled with damp peat moss and store them for several months in the vegetable compartment of your refrigerator. Kiwi fruit seeds should remain in the fruit during the stratification process.

Germinate seeds in a nursery flat filled with sterile potting soil. Most seeds should be planted just below the soil surface. Covering the flat with clear plastic or a piece of glass will help maintain the high humidity necessary for germination. But be careful: Too much moisture encourages soil diseases that can attack seeds and seedlings. Germination time varies by plant.

Most subtropical fruit seeds will remain viable for several months, but some seeds, such as citrus, litchi, and mango, are quite perishable once they have been removed from the fruit. Mango seeds are enclosed in a husk that must be removed before planting. Also, the seeds will not be viable if the fruit has been stored at a temperature below 55° F.

Grafting and Budding
Budding and grafting are vegetative propagation techniques in which a piece of stem or a single bud of a selected variety (scion) is fused with a rootstock. To be successful, the cambium areas (a thin layer of growing tissue beneath the bark) of the scion and the rootstock must be in contact. Formation of callus (a hard, white tissue) at the union between the scion and the rootstock is a sign that the bud or graft is "taking."

Deciduous plants are grafted while dormant. Evergreen plants are usually grafted in the spring. Each piece of scion must have at least one well-developed but dormant bud. High humidity and warm temperatures (common greenhouse conditions) favor successful grafting.

Macadamia and mango scion wood should be wrapped tightly with a piece of wire several weeks prior to cutting it from the mother tree. This girdling forces the scion wood to store food and stimulates development of latent buds.

Budding is probably the easiest grafting method. It allows a large number of plants to be propagated from a small amount of scion wood. It is also suitable for larger trunks and stems. Budding can be done whenever the bark is slipping (when it separates easily from the cambium). This is usually in the spring, when plants are actively growing, but budding can also be done in summer and fall. The most common forms of budding are illustrated on page 87.

Although a variety of specialized grafting tools are available, you can make do with a sharp pocketknife, grafting tape, a good pair of pruning shears, and a can of commercially available grafting sealer. You may also need a small cleaver, a hammer and nails, and a pruning saw for grafting large limbs.

Rooting Softwood and Semihardwood Cuttings

Softwood

Tear off leaves

Semihardwood

Hardwood

1. *Remove leaves from bottom 3 inches of cutting.*
2. *Slice a strip of bark* from each side of base.
3. *Dip end of cutting in rooting hormone and plant* in rooting medium.
4. *Cover with plastic to maintain humidity.*

Air-Layering

Scrape away cambium

Plastic wrap

Twist tie

1. *Remove a ring of bark an inch wide and scrape away the cambium layer.*
2. *Cover the ring with slightly moist sphagnum moss and plastic wrap.*
3. *When roots have filled the moss, cut the shoot and plant the new tree.*

Rooting Cuttings

Cuttings are short pieces of stem that are removed from a plant and stimulated to form roots at the basal end. There are three types of vegetative cuttings, but they differ only in the maturity of the growth being propagated. A cutting taken from new growth at the tip of a branch is referred to as a *softwood cutting*; one taken from growth that is six to eight weeks old is described as a *semihardwood cutting*; and a section taken from the oldest growth of the current or past season (if the plant is dormant) is termed a *hardwood cutting*.

Subtropical fruit that can be propagated by cuttings may form roots on a softwood cutting but not a hardwood cutting, or vice versa. So it's very important to take cuttings at the right time and from the right place. Use a rooting hormone according to the label directions to help stimulate root development on the basal end of the cutting. Let as many leaves remain on the cutting as is practical, and maintain high humidity. A 60-40 mix of perlite and peat moss is a popular rooting medium for subtropical fruit. Keep the temperature of the medium between 75° and 85° F with one of the heating systems designed for plant propagation.

Dividing Plants

Bananas cannot be propagated by rooting cuttings, grafting, or air-layering, but they do produce suckers or offshoots identical to the mother plant, which can be removed and rooted. Remove as large a piece of the mother root as possible when removing the offshoot; small shoots may not have enough stored food to establish new roots. Remove one third to one half of the foliage from the division, tie the remaining leaves together, and plant it in warm soil. Maintain high humidity to keep shoots from drying out.

Air-Layering

Litchis are best propagated by air-layering. In this method, a shoot is partially severed from the parent plant and forced to grow roots. After the shoot is rooted, it is removed from the parent and planted. See page 86 for an illustrated description of this technique.

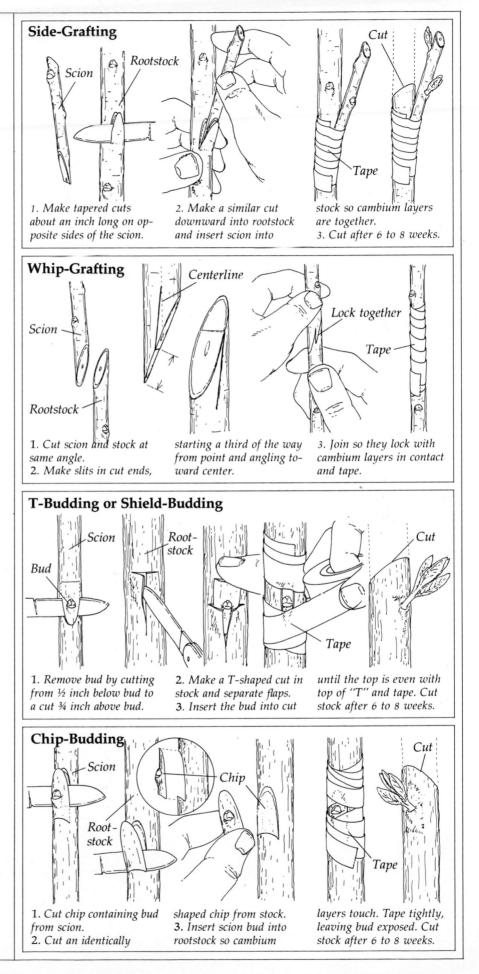

Side-Grafting

Scion *Rootstock* *Cut* *Tape*

1. Make tapered cuts about an inch long on opposite sides of the scion.
2. Make a similar cut downward into rootstock and insert scion into stock so cambium layers are together.
3. Cut after 6 to 8 weeks.

Whip-Grafting

Centerline *Scion* *Rootstock* *Lock together* *Tape*

1. Cut scion and stock at same angle.
2. Make slits in cut ends, starting a third of the way from point and angling toward center.
3. Join so they lock with cambium layers in contact and tape.

T-Budding or Shield-Budding

Scion *Rootstock* *Bud* *Cut* *Tape*

1. Remove bud by cutting from ½ inch below bud to a cut ¾ inch above bud.
2. Make a T-shaped cut in stock and separate flaps.
3. Insert the bud into cut until the top is even with top of "T" and tape. Cut stock after 6 to 8 weeks.

Chip-Budding

Scion *Rootstock* *Chip* *Cut* *Tape*

1. Cut chip containing bud from scion.
2. Cut an identically shaped chip from stock.
3. Insert scion bud into rootstock so cambium layers touch. Tape tightly, leaving bud exposed. Cut stock after 6 to 8 weeks.

Subtropical Fruits in Containers

Container plantings offer the gardener versatility and opportunity.
Many plants that would not survive if planted in the garden will thrive in
containers—indoors and out.

Growing subtropical fruits in containers solves many otherwise insurmountable problems of soil, site, and climate. If the soil in your yard is poorly drained, you can fill a container with a soil mix that will provide excellent aeration, moisture-holding capacity, and drainage. You may not have a place in your yard with sunlight suitable for year-round cultivation of a particular species, but if the plants are in containers they can be moved about as the weather dictates. But most of all, if you live in a cold climate, you can enjoy many of the species in this book that would not survive a winter outdoors. Containers are wonderfully mobile. They can be moved indoors or to greenhouses for protection from the coldest winters and then back outdoors when the weather is right.

Container culture is also one of the most attractive ways to enjoy subtropical fruits. Matched with a handsome pot that complements their distinctive habit, they can be moved to center stage when in fruit or flower, then shuttled back to the best growing area as needed.

What Type of Container?
When choosing a container, consider its size, durability, and weight.

Left: *Many subtropicals are well suited for container culture indoors, outdoors, or in solariums. From left to right: banana, 'Chinotto' sour orange, and calamondin.*

Right: *'Marsh' grapefruit*

A small plant, such as a calamondin, can be grown for years in a gallon-sized pot. Many others should be moved to ever larger containers until a 15-gallon size is reached. Containers larger than 15 gallons are unwieldy and difficult to move.

Large clay, stone, and ceramic containers are very durable but can be heavy. Wood containers are attractive and generally lightweight. Unless treated with a nontoxic preservative, however, the constant contact with wet soil causes them to rot quickly. Plastic containers are light and durable and are available in many designs.

Container Soils
The ideal container soil combines optimal aeration and drainage with good moisture retention and the ability to hold an available supply of necessary nutrients. It should also be lightweight so that the containers can be moved easily. Garden soils are not good container soils. They rarely drain properly, are usually too heavy, and often contain disease organisms. Instead, use one of the many potting soils available in nurseries, or mix your own using the following recipe.

To make about 1 cubic yard of soil, take:
- 14 cubic feet of peat moss or composted fir or pine bark
- 14 cubic feet of perlite

Dump the ingredients in a pile and roughly mix them. Dampen the mix as you go. Dry peat moss is far easier to wet with warm water than with cool water.

Spread these fertilizers over the rough mix:
- 5 pounds of ground limestone
- 5 pounds of 5-10-10 fertilizer containing calcium, magnesium, sulfur, iron, manganese, and zinc.

Mix by shoveling (use a scoop shovel) the ingredients into a cone-shaped pile, letting each shovelful dribble down the cone. To get a thoroughly mixed product, the cone-building should be repeated three to five times.

If you are not going to use the mix right away, store it in plastic bags or plastic garbage cans. To mix smaller quantities, reduce the amounts of the ingredients proportionately. The nutrients in the mix will last about three to four weeks.

Then, begin fertilizing according to the instructions in "Fertilizing Plants in Containers," at right.

Watering Plants in Containers

Plants grown in containers require more frequent watering than those grown in the ground. Dark-colored containers will dry out faster than light-colored ones, and porous pots made of wood or clay will dry out faster than those of nonporous plastic.

Apply enough water so the entire rootball becomes wet. This may take several passes with the hose. Make sure the water is not just running down the space between the rootball and container, a common occurrence if the plant has gone too long without water.

In areas with salty water, such as the Southwest, be sure to leach the soil well by adding enough water so that 10 to 20 percent of the water applied drains from the bottom of the container.

You can get a good idea as to whether a plant needs water by gently tipping its container. If it feels light, the plant needs water; if it feels heavy, the plant can probably go a while longer.

Fertilizing Plants in Containers

Frequent watering leaches nutrients rapidly. To compensate, fertilize once a month with a liquid fertilizer according to the instructions on the label. Begin in early spring and stop in late summer or early fall to avoid encouraging late, frost-sensitive growth. Fast-growing plants such as bananas may need more frequent feeding. Micronutrients can also be leached quickly from container soils, so use a complete fertilizer containing micronutrients.

Root Pruning

Sooner or later your plants—even those well adapted to containers—will begin to run out of root space. When this happens, the dense rootball becomes harder to water, the plant grows slowly, and fruit production declines. A solution, although it may seem a drastic one, is to prune the roots. First, and this is the most important step, prune the top of the plant, reducing its size by at least one third. This compensates for the roots you are about to prune off. Next, remove the plant from the container and cut off one fourth to one third of the outside of the rootball with a sharp knife. Then place the plant back in the container with fresh soil, and water thoroughly. When done properly, root pruning quickly invigorates rootbound plants.

Removing a large plant from a big container can be difficult. You'll probably need help. A better idea is to plan ahead, and build a container with sides that are easily removed. With a little creative carpentry you can build functional and attractive containers with slip-away sides or removal bolts.

Below: 'Meyer' lemons are popular container plants because they bloom over a long period and bear bumper crops on small, compact trees.

Growing Subtropical Fruits in Cold Climates

Tender fruiting plants, such as bananas, papayas, and figs, have been grown in cold climates for centuries. Orangeries, large greenhouses for overwintering containerized citrus, date back to sixteenth-century Europe. Some small-fruited types of citrus, such as calamondin and the 'Otaheite' orange, have been popular American houseplants for decades.

Today, perhaps because of the increased use of greenhouses for solar heating, subtropical fruits are becoming more popular in colder climates. New organizations and clubs reflect this surge of interest. For example, the Indoor Citrus and Rare Fruit Society (IC&RFS) is a growing organization "dedicated to the development and enjoyment of indoor/outdoor fruit culture." Its quarterly newsletter provides information on growing all types of tropical and subtropical fruit, indoors and outdoors. See page 94 for the group's address.

Many of the common rules change when you move subtropical fruit indoors, whether it's into a greenhouse, into a cool basement, or onto a sunny windowsill. It can't be denied that many of these plants will need pampering and will require much more effort than the average houseplant.

The rewards are there as well, however. In one of their newsletters, a member of the IC&RFS wrote, "My wife and I are as contrary as any other Americans, and one form that our contrariness takes is the joy at seeing the calamondin orange on our bedroom windowsill when snow is falling outside. There it is, a summer thing, a tropic thing, mocking the elements with orange-colored ripe fruit, green fruit, an abundance of evergreen leaves, and blossoms breathing the citrus fragrance called neroli. This orange tree, although no more than 2 feet high and 2 feet in branch span, is nearly thirty years old, and for most of its life has flourished. Like chives in a kitchen pot, oranges are there for the picking, almost all year round. The calamondin has brought so much joyous promise of new growth in the midst of winter—when snows are blowing or temperatures are below zero—that I can no longer imagine a house without at least one citrus on a sunny windowsill."

Providing the Best Conditions

You'll have to follow a few rules for growing subtropical fruit in cold climates, especially if you expect to enjoy fresh fruit. Each plant will require different conditions. Some are best grown in warm greenhouses the year around. Others should be grown outdoors in the summer, then moved to a cool but frost-free location in the winter.

Despite these variations, a few guidelines apply to all containerized tropicals.

Make Smooth Transitions
Take your time moving plants from one location to another. If you're moving plants outside after a long winter indoors, do it gradually. Place them in a shady spot first. Then slowly give the plants more sun over a period of several weeks. This will help prevent sunburned foliage. Also, watch out for late spring frosts.

Moving plants from outdoors to indoors should be done at an equally slow pace. Give the plant less and less sun until it's ready to come inside. Before bringing it indoors, hose it down to wash off any dust or dirt on the leaves. If necessary, spray to control pests.

Right: *Citrus trees bring color indoors when its needed most—in the midst of winter. Here are 'Eureka' lemon (right) and 'Fairchild' mandarin (left).*

Maintain High Humidity

The dry heat that circulates through most homes during the cold months of the year will severely shock plants that have been outside all summer. This usually means they lose all their leaves. Do everything possible to increase the humidity around the plants: Spray the foliage with a fine mist of water, place the containers on a tray of rocks partially submerged in water, group the plants so they can humidify each other, or buy a humidifier. Also, keep plants away from heater vents.

Adjust Care to Conditions

Once plants are indoors they won't need as much water, but don't allow them to dry out completely. If you are just trying to keep plants cool and dormant until spring, they won't need much light either. If you are trying to ripen fruit, however, the more light the better. You may want to consider supplemental illumination with artificial lights. Adjust your feedings according to how you want the plant to grow, but in general feed lightly, if at all.

Which Fruit To Try?

Almost any plant can be grown in a container if the pot is large enough. Some plants, however, adapt better to container growing. Most of them are small, so moving them to ever larger pots is done at a leisurely pace, and they won't get so large that they are difficult to move. Bananas, dwarf citrus, figs, guavas, pineapple guavas, loquat, papaya, passion fruit, and tree tomatoes are all perfectly suited to containers.

Banana

The banana's fast growth rate makes it a good choice for indoor/outdoor culture or for growing in a greenhouse the year around. Conditions must be exact to ripen fruit, however—as hot and sunny as possible with high humidity. The only sure way to produce these conditions is to put the plant in a greenhouse. You also need to watch soil moisture levels. A fast-growing plant, such as a banana plant, in a warm location needs lots of water. Conversely, if the conditions are cool, be careful not to overwater.

Choose dwarf varieties. If everything goes according to plan, they can bear fruit within 18 months of planting.

Dwarf Citrus

More types of citrus are grown in cold climates than any other subtropical fruit. Many are grown indoors in winter and outdoors in summer. Others are grown in greenhouses or sunny windows the year around.

Acid citrus types, such as lemons, calamondins, and limes, are most popular, simply because they tend to be ever-blooming, don't need heat to sweeten them, and ripen in a relatively short time. If you have a greenhouse, however, almost anything is possible.

You can treat citrus a number of different ways. If the trees are kept in a cool location, below 55° F, they will remain dormant but the fruit will still ripen. This is usually the least stressful way of overwintering the trees. If you keep them warmer, many will continue to grow and bloom during the winter, but you must supply light and high humidity for healthy growth. In this case, a greenhouse is ideal.

Any citrus grown indoors will have a greater chance of setting fruit if hand-pollinated. Simply use a small artist's brush to spread pollen from one flower to another.

Top: *These are ideal conditions for growing citrus indoors—bright light from a large window and increased humidity from running water.*

Bottom: *Containers made of redwood are long lasting and make a handsome addition to a patio or deck.*

Feijoa

The pineapple guava is one of the most rugged subtropical plants. If the plant is kept cool (45° to 55° F) in winter it will remain dormant and will flower when taken outdoors the following spring. The fruit ripen in midsummer, usually about four months after flowers open. The feijoa can also be grown in a greenhouse.

Fig

The fig is the easiest subtropical fruit to grow in cold climates. It is deciduous and relatively hardy, and in many areas it can be overwintered if covered with a thick mulch, or protected as illustrated on page 13. Also, it bears two crops and often bears fruit the first year after planting. A plant grown in a container can simply be moved to a garage, greenhouse, or basement and brought back outside when the weather warms.

Guava

Both the tropical and the strawberry guava can be overwintered indoors, but the strawberry guava is more adaptable and can more easily withstand the rigors of dramatically changing conditions. It is also more likely to be ever-blooming, and the fruit ripens over a shorter period. Treat guavas as you would citrus plants, but prune them regularly to keep them compact. The tropical guava is best adapted to hot, humid greenhouse conditions.

Loquat

The loquat is one of the easier plants to bring to fruit indoors. It grows well under a variety of indoor conditions and is sometimes sold as a houseplant. The plant blooms in the fall and, if it is kept cool after the fruit set, the fruit should ripen the following spring. For best results, grow the loquat outdoors in summer and prune the plant in spring to keep it compact.

Papaya

The papaya is best grown in a greenhouse the year around; it is unlikely it would survive without 12 months of high heat and humidity. If you can provide these conditions, your chances of enjoying fruit are good. Just remember to plant at least three seeds to ensure the presence of male and female flowers for pollination. (See page 65 for more about papaya flowers.) Low-growing varieties of Hawaiian papaya, such as 'Solo', are best.

Passion Fruit

The passion fruit vine is a handsome addition to a greenhouse or to a patio in the summer. Flowering is triggered by day length and seems to be more prolific when the roots are cramped in a container. Fruit set is most likely under humid conditions. The fruit ripens three to four months after flowering. Prune to keep the plant within bounds. Although the vine will grow indoors, it will seldom flower or set fruit in the low light.

Tree Tomato

The tree tomato and its relatives in the *Solanaceae* family are good indoor/outdoor plants for cold climates. They grow quickly from seed, fruit at a young age, and adapt well to a variety of indoor conditions.

How to Move Large Container Plants

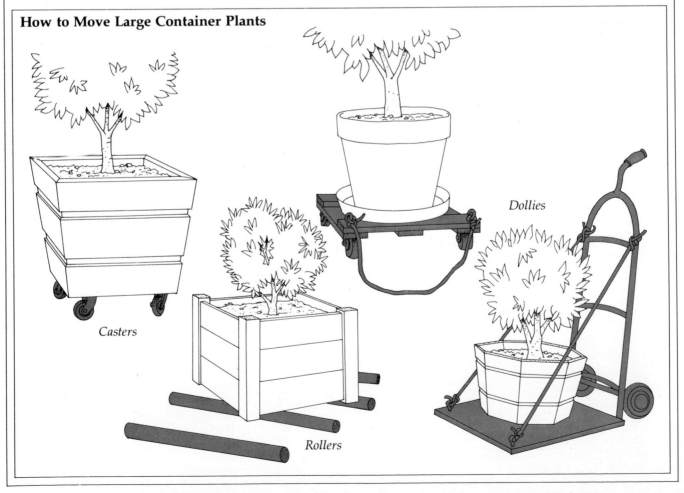

Casters

Rollers

Dollies

Plant and Seed Suppliers

	Catalog Price	Papaya	Feijoa	Citrus	Avocado	Kiwi Fruit	Fig	Passion Fruit	Pomegranate	Mango	Cherimoya	Banana	Guava	Litchi	Tree Tomato	Sapote
A LOGEE'S GREENHOUSES 55 North Street Danielson, CT 06239	$3			•			•	•				•				
B ALBERTS & MERKEL 2210 South Federal Highway Boynton Beach, FL 33435	Free			•			•		•							
C ADAMS CITRUS NURSERIES 2020 Dundee Road Winter Haven, FL 33880	Free			•												
D LOUISIANA NURSERY Route 7, Box 43 Opelousas, LA 70570	Free						•		•							
E PLANT KINGDOM Box 7273 Lincoln Acres, CA 92083	50¢	•	•				•	•	•	•	•	•	•	•	•	•
F NORTHWOODS NURSERY 28696 South Gramer Road Molalla, OR 97038	Free					•	•		•							
G PATRICKS NURSERY Box 1590 Ty Ty, GA 31795	Free						•		•							
H EASTVILLE PLANTATION Box 337 Bogart, GA 30622	Free					•	•		•							
I EXOTICA SEED CO. & RARE FRUIT NURSERY 2508 East Vista Way Vista, CA 92083	$2	•	•	•	•	•	•	•	•	•	•	•	•	•	•	•
J STARK BROTHERS NURSERIES Louisiana, MO 63353-0010	Free						•		•							
K HASTINGS Box 4274 Atlanta, GA 30303-4274	Free					•	•		•							
L RAINTREE NURSERY 391 Butts Road Morton, WA 98356	Free			•		•	•		•							
M FOUR WINDS GROWERS Box 3538 Fremont, CA 94539	Free			•	•											
N EDIBLE LANDSCAPING Route 2, Box 343 A Afton, VA 22920	$1					•	•		•							
O PACIFIC TREE FARMS 4301 Lynwood Drive Chula Vista, CA 92010	$1.50	•	•	•	•	•	•	•	•	•	•	•	•	•	•	•
P GARDEN OF DELIGHTS 2018 Mayo Street Hollywood, FL 33020	Free	•	•	•	•		•	•		•	•	•	•			•
Q LYCHEE TREE NURSERY 3151 South Kanner Highway Stuart, FL 33494	Free	•	•	•												•
R CARMAN'S NURSERY 16201 Mozart Avenue Los Gatos, CA 95030	Free		•			•	•	•	•							
S MAR VISTA NURSERY Box 1056 Carpinteria, CA 93013	50¢	•	•			•	•	•	•	•	•	•				•
T JERSEY CHESTNUT FARM 58 Van Duyne Avenue Wayne, NJ 07470	Free															
U POSSUM TROT TROPICAL NURSERY 14955 S.W. 214th Street Miami, FL 33187	Free	•	•	•	•			•		•	•	•				•
V THE FIG TREE NURSERY Box 124 Gulf Hammock, FL 32639	50¢						•									
W W.O. LESSARD NURSERY 19201 S.W. 248th Street Homestead, FL 33031	50¢											•				
X THE BANANA TREE 715 Northampton Street Easton, PA 18042	Free											•				
Y BROKAW NURSERY Box 4818 Saticoy, CA 93003	Free	•	•	•	•			•		•	•		•	•	•	•

Information Sources

1 **CALIFORNIA RARE FRUIT GROWERS, INC.**
The Fullerton Arboretum
California State University, Fullerton
Fullerton, CA 92634
Membership fee: $10

2 **RARE FRUIT COUNCIL INTERNATIONAL, INC.**
13609 Old Cutler Road
Miami, FL 33158
Membership fee: $20

3 **NORTH AMERICAN FRUIT EXPLORERS**
Mary Kurle, Membership Chairperson
10 South 055 Madison Street
Hinsdale, IL 60521
Membership fee: $6

4 **CALIFORNIA AVOCADO SOCIETY**
Box 4816
Saticoy, CA 93004
Membership fee: $10

5 **NORTHERN NUT GROWERS ASSOCIATION**
Ken Bauman, Treasurer
9870 South Palmer Road
New Carlisle, OH 45344
Membership fee: $13

6 **CALIFORNIA MACADAMIA SOCIETY**
Box 1290
Fallbrook, CA 92028
Membership fee: $12.50

7 **KIWIFRUIT GROWERS OF CALIFORNIA, INC.**
1151 Los Rios Drive
Carmichael, CA 95608
Membership fee: $30

8 **AMERICAN SOCIETY FOR HORTICULTURAL SCIENCE**
701 North Saint Asaph Street
Alexandria, VA 22314
Membership fee: $50

9 **HOME ORCHARD SOCIETY**
2511 S.W. Miles Street
Portland, OR 97219
Membership fee: $5

10 **FRIENDS OF THE FIG SOCIETY**
840 Ralph Road
Conyers, GA 30208
Membership fee: $5

11 **AMERICAN POMOLOGICAL SOCIETY**
103 Tyson Building
University Park, PA 16802
Membership fee: $12

12 **INTERNATIONAL DWARF FRUIT TREE ASSOCIATION**
301 Horticulture Building
Michigan State University
East Lansing, MI 48824
Membership fee: $25

13 **FLORIDA STATE HORTICULTURAL SOCIETY**
800 Lake Jessie Drive
Winter Haven, FL 33880
Membership fee: $15

14 **INDOOR CITRUS & RARE FRUIT SOCIETY**
176 Coronado Avenue
Los Altos, CA 94022
Membership fee: $10

Note: Page numbers in italics refer to illustrations.

A
Acerola cherry, 74
Actinidia arguta, 55
Actinidia chinensis. See Kiwi fruit
Actinidia kolomikta, 55
Adaptation
  avocado, 16
  banana, 20–21
  cherimoya, 23–24
  citrus, 27–28
  feijoa, 44–45
  fig, 46
  guava, 49–50
  kiwi, 51–52
  litchi, 55
  loquat, 57
  macadamia, 59
  mango, 62
  papaya, 65
  passion vine, 67
  persimmon, 68
  tree tomato, 72
  white sapote, 70
Air-layering, 87
Alligator pear. *See* Avocado(s)
Ananas comosus, 73
Animal pests, 85
Annona cherimola. See
  Cherimoya(s)
Annona muricata, 25
Annona squamosa, 25
Anthracnose, 84, 85
Aphids, 82, 83
Apple-Banana Bread, 23
Arizona, citrus for, 27
Asimina triloba, 73
Atemoya, 5, 25
Australian nut. *See*
  Macadamia(s)
Averrhoa carambola, 73
Avocado(s), 16–19
  Soup, 19
  varieties, 19

B
Banana(s), 20–23, 92
  Bread, Apple-, 23
  Butter, Special Pink, 22
  in cold climate, 88, 92
  in containers, 88, 92
  Sorbet, Tropical, 23
  varieties, 21
Basin, watering, 76, 79, 80
Bergamot, 27
Birds, 85
Bloom, citrus, 28
Bread, Apple-Banana, 23
Budding, grafting and, 86, 87
Butter, Special Pink Banana, 22

C
Cake
  Persimmon, 70
  Sweet Orange and Almond,
    39–40
California
  avocados for, 19
  citrus for, 27, 41–43
  macadamias for, 60
  mangoes for, 64
Capulin cherry, 75
Carica species. *See* Papaya(s)
Carissa macrocarpa, 73
Carob, 73
Casimiroa edulis. See Sapote,
  white
Caterpillars, 82–83
Ceratonia siliqua, 73
Cherimoya(s), 23–25
  relatives, 25
  varieties, 25

Cherry of the Rio Grande, 6, 73
Chicken With Macadamia-
  Mango Stuffing, 60, 61
Chilling requirements, 10
Chutney
  Mango, 64
  papaya, 66
Citrange, 30
Citrangequat, 28
Citron, 29, 32, 43
Citrus, 7, 26, 27
  See also specific fruits
  adaptation, 27–28
  in cold climate, 92
  dwarf, 92
  fruit shape, 28
  fruit size, 27, 28
  harvesting and storing, 31
  pollination, 29
  propagation, 29–30
  relatives, 40
  rootstocks, 30
  site selection and planting, 30
  tree habit 29
  trees, 4, 7, 31
  trees, caring for, 30–31
  types of, 32–40
  varieties, 41–43
Clausena lansium. See Wampi
Climate, 9–13
  cold, 9, 91–92
  effects on citrus, 28–29
  and fertilizing, 80
  regions, 10–11
  variables, 9–10
  and watering, 79
Coffea arabica, 73
Coffee, 73
Cold
  climate, 91–92
  protection, 12–13
  tolerance, 9
Color, citrus, 28–29
Container(s), 88, 89
  avocados for, 19
  choosing, 89
  choosing plants for, 92–93
  fertilizing plants in, 90
  planting from, 78
  pruning roots for, 90
  soil for, 89–90
  watering plants in, 90
Cultivars, 15
Cuttings, rooting, 87
Cyphomandra betacea. See Tree
  tomato(es)

D
Deserts, citrus for, 27, 41–43
Diospyros digyna. See Sapote,
  black
Diospyros kaki. See
  Persimmon(s), Oriental
Diospyros virginiana. See
  Persimmon(s), American
Diseases, 84–85. *See also* Pests
  and diseases
Dividing plants, 87
Dovyalis caffra, 73
Drip systems, 80

E
Eriobotrya japonica. See Loquat(s)
Eugenia aggregata, 6, 74, 74
Eugenia brasiliensis, 6, 74, 74
Eugenia luschnathiana, 6, 74, 74
Eugenia uniflora, 6, 74
Euphoria longan, 74, 74
Exposure, 12

F
Feijoa(s), 44–45
  in cold climate, 93
  varieties, 45

Fertilizers, 80–81
Fertilizing, 80–81
  avocado trees, 17
  banana plants, 22
  cherimoya trees, 25
  citrus trees, 30, 31
  container plants, 90
  feijoa plants, 45
  fig trees, 47–48
  guava plants, 50
  kiwi vines, 52
  litchi trees, 56
  loquat trees, 58
  macadamia trees, 60
  mango trees, 62
  papaya plants, 65
  passion vines, 67
  persimmon trees, 69
  tree tomato, 72
  white sapote, 71
Ficus carica. See Fig(s)
Fig(s), 46–48
  in cold climate, 93
  Spiced, 48
  varieties, 47
Fireblight, 84–85, 85
Florida
  avocados for, 19
  citrus for, 28, 41–43
  mango for, 62, 63
Fortunella species. *See*
  Kumquat(s)

G
Garcinia mangostana, 74
Grafting and budding, 86, 87
Granadilla. *See* Passion fruit
Grapefruit(s), 29, 32–33
  in containers, 89
  size, 27
  varieties, 43
Grumichama, 6, 74
Guacamole, 18, 19
Guava(s), 10, 49–50
  in cold climate, 93
  Jelly, 50
  pineapple. *See* Feijoa(s)
  varieties, 50
Gulf Coast, citrus for, 27, 41–43

H
Harvesting and storing
  avocados, 18
  bananas, 22
  cherimoyas, 25
  citrus, 31
  feijoas, 45
  figs, 48
  guavas, 50
  kiwis, 54–55
  litchis, 57
  loquats, 58
  macadamias, 60–61
  mangoes, 63
  papayas, 66
  passion fruit, 67
  persimmons, 69
  tree tomato, 72
  white sapote, 71
Hawaii
  avocados for, 19
  macadamias for, 60
  mangoes for, 63
Heat requirements, 9
Houseplants, 91–93
Hovenia juicina, 74
How to Build & Use Greenhouses,
  85
How to use this book, 7
Humidity, 9
  indoors, 92

I
Indoor Citrus and Rare Fruit
  Society, 91
Indoor plants, 91–93
Insects, 82–84. *See also* Pests and
  diseases

J
Jaboticaba, 75, 75
Japanese
  medlar. *See* Loquat(s)
  persimmon. *See*
    Persimmon(s), Oriental
  plum. *See* Loquat(s)
Jelly, Guava, 50
Juice, citrus, 29
Jujube, 75

K
Kei apple, 73
Key lime pie, 36
Kiwi fruit, 51–55
  female varieties, 54
  hardy, 55
  male varieties, 55
  relatives, 55
Kumquat(s), 28, 33–34
  See also Citrus
  hybrids, 33
  Sauce, Roast Duck With,
    33–34
  size, 27
  varieties, 43

L
Landscape design, 5–6
Leaf spots, 84, 85
Leather, Mango, 63
Lemon(s), 28, 34–35
  See also Citrus
  container plant, 90, 91
  indoors, 91
  Pork, Southern Style, 35–36
  size, 27
  trees, 4, 12, 30, 90
  varieties, 42
Lime(s), 26, 28, 35–36
  See also Citrus
  Curd Tart, 36
  pie, 36
  size, 27
  varieties, 43
Limequat(s), 28, 33
  See also Citrus
  variety, 43
Litchi(s), 55–57
  dried, 57
Longan, 74, 74
Loquat(s), 57–58
  in cold climate, 93
  dried, 58
  Sauce, Spicy, 58
  varieties, 58
Love fruit. *See* Avocado(s)

M
Macadamia(s), 59–61
  -Mango Stuffing, Chicken
    With, 60, 61
  varieties, 60
Malabar chestnut, 75
Malpighia glabra, 74
Mandarin(s), 28–29, 36–37
  See also Citrus
  hybrids, 36
  size, 27
  trees, indoors, 91
  varieties, 42
Mangifera indica. See Mango(es)
Mango(es), 61–64
  Chutney, 64
  Leather, 63
  Stuffing, Chicken With
    Macadamia-, 60, 61
  varieties, 62, 63, 64

Mangosteen, 74
Manilkara zapota, 74
Maturity, citrus, 28
Mealybugs, 83
Medlar, Japanese. *See* Loquat(s)
Melon pear, 72
Melon shrub, 72
Mexican apple. *See* Sapote, white
Microclimates, 11
Micronutrients, 81
Miracle fruit, 75, 75
Mites, 83, 84
Morus nigra, 74
Mulberry, black, 74
Mulches, 79–80, 81–82
Murraya paniculata. See Orange jessamine
Musa species. *See* Banana(s)
Myrciaria cauliflora, 75, 75

N
Natal plum, 73
Nematodes, 83
Nurseries
    choosing plants at, 77
    names and addresses, 94
Nuts. *See* Litchi(s), dried; Macadamia(s)

O
Opuntia ficus-indica, 75, 75
Orange(s), 38
    See also Citrus
    and Almond Cake, Sweet, 39–40
    blood, 27, 28, 38–39, 41
    common, 29, 38, 39, 39, 41
    in containers, 88
    jessamine, 40
    mandarin. *See* Mandarin(s)
    navel, 27, 29, 38, 39, 41
    size, 27
    sour, 27, 29, 38, 40, 41
    at the table, 38–39
    trees, 4
    trifoliate, 7, 30, 40, 40
    varieties, 41
Orangequat, 43. *See also* Citrus
Organizations, names and addresses, 94
Oriental persimmon. *See* Persimmon(s), Oriental

P
Pachira aquatica, 75
Papaya(s), 64–66
    in cold climate, 93
Passiflora species. *See* Passion fruit
Passion fruit, 6, 66–68
    in cold climate, 93
    varieties, 67
Pawpaw, 73
Pear-melon, 72
Peel, citrus, 28
Pepino, 72
Persea americana. See Avocado(s)
Persimmon(s)
    American, 68, 69–70
    Cake, 70
    Japanese. *See* Persimmon(s), Oriental
    Oriental, 68–69, 70
        relatives, 69–70
        varieties, 69
Pests and diseases, 82–85
    avocado, 18
    banana, 22
    cherimoya, 25
    citrus, 30–31
    feijoa plants, 45
    fig tree, 48

guava plants, 50
kiwi vines, 54
litchi trees, 56
loquat trees, 58
macadamia trees, 60
mango trees, 62–63
papaya plants, 65–66
passion vines, 67
persimmon trees, 69
tree tomato, 72
white sapote, 71
Pie, Key lime, 36
Pineapple, 75
Pitomba, 6, 74
Plantains. *See* Banana(s)
Planting, 79. *See also* Site selection and planting
Plant Propagation, Principles and Practices, 85
Plum
    Japanese. *See* Loquat(s)
    natal, 73
Pollination, 15
    avocado, 16–17
    banana, 21
    cherimoya, 23, 24–25
    citrus, 29
    guava, 50
    kiwis, 52
    litchi, 56
    mango, 62
    papaya, 65
    persimmons, 68
Poncirus trifoliata. See Orange(s), trifoliate
Prickly pear, 75, 75
Propagation, 85
    avocado, 17
    banana, 23
    citrus, 29–30
    feijoa, 45
    fig, 47
    kiwi, 52
    litchi, 56
    loquat, 58
    macadamia, 60
    mango, 62
    papaya, 65
    passion vines, 67
    persimmons, 68
    white sapote, 70
Pruning, 82
    avocado trees, 17–18
    banana plants, 22
    cherimoya trees, 25
    citrus trees, 30
    feijoa plants, 45
    fig trees, 48
    guava plants, 50
    kiwi vines, 52–54
    litchi trees, 56
    loquat trees, 58
    macadamia trees, 60
    mango trees, 62
    papaya plants, 65
    passion vines, 67
    persimmon trees, 69
    root, 90
    tree tomato, 72
    white sapote, 71
Prunus salicifolia, 75
Psidium species. *See* Guava(s)
Pummelo(s), 29, 40
    size, 27
    variety, 43

Q
Queensland nut. *See* Macadamia(s)

R
Radiation, sunlight, 11–12
Rainfall, 9
Raisin tree, 74

Recipes
    Apple-Banana Bread, 23
    Avocado Soup, 19
    Chicken With Macadamia-Mango Stuffing, 60, 61
    Guava Jelly, 50
    Lemon Pork, Southern Style, 35–36
    Lime Curd Tart, 36
    Mango Chutney, 64
    Mango Leather, 63
    Persimmon Cake, 70
    Roast Duck With Kumquat Sauce, 33–34
    Special Pink Banana Butter, 22
    Spiced Figs, 48
    Spicy Loquat Sauce, 58
    Sweet Orange and Almond Cake, 39–40
    Tropical Banana Sorbet, 23
    White Sapote Crumb Squares, 71
Roast Duck With Kumquat Sauce, 33–34
Rodents, 85
Rootstocks, citrus, 30

S
Saccharum officinarum, 75
Sapodilla, 74
Sapote, black, 70
Sapote, white, 71–72
    Crumb Squares, 72
    varieties, 72
Sauce
    Roast Duck With Kumquat, 33–34
    Spicy Loquat, 58
Scale, 83, 84
Seed, growing plants from, 85–86
Semitropical climates, 10
Site selection and planting
    avocado, 17
    banana, 21
    cherimoya, 25
    citrus, 30
    feijoa, 45
    figs, 47
    guavas, 50
    kiwis, 52
    litchis, 56
    loquats, 58
    macadamia, 60
    mango, 62
    papaya, 65
    passion vines, 67
    persimmons, 68–69
    tree tomato, 72
    white sapote, 70
Slugs, 84
Smudge pots, 10
Snails, 84
Societies, names and addresses, 94
Soil, 77–79
    for containers, 89–90
    and fertilizing, 80
    and watering, 79
Solanum muricatum, 72
Sorbet, Tropical Banana, 23
Soup, Avocado, 19
Sources of plants and information, 94
Soursop, 25
Special Pink Banana Butter, 22
Spiced Figs, 48
Spicy Loquat Sauce, 58
Sprinklers, 80
Star fruit, 73
Storing. *See* Harvesting and storing

Stuffing, Chicken With Macadamia-Mango, 60, 61
Subtropical climates, 10–11
Subtropical fruits, 5
    See also specific fruits
    caring for, 77–87
    chart, 73–75
    choosing, 15
    in containers, 88, 89–92
    encyclopedia of, 15–75
    flavors, 15
    harvest periods, 15
    plants, choosing, 77
    pollination, 15
    propagation, 85
    reasons for growing, 5–7
    selected varieties, 15
    at the table, 6–7
Sugar apple, 25
Sugar cane, 75
Sunlight, 10, 11–12
Surinam cherry, 6, 74
Sweet Orange and Almond Cake, 39–40
Sweetsop, 25
Synsepalum dulcificum, 75, 75

T
Tamarillo. *See* Tree tomato(es)
Tamarind, 75, 75
Tangelo(s), 28, 36, 37
    See also Citrus
    size, 27
    trees, 4
    varieties, 43
Tangor(s), 37
    See also Citrus
    varieties, 43
Tara vine, 55
Tart, Lime Curd, 36
Temperate climates, 11
Texas, citrus for, 27
Thrips, 84, 85
Tomatoes, tree. *See* Tree tomato(es)
Tree tomato(es), 70
    in cold climate, 93
    relatives, 71
Tropical
    climates, 10
    landscape, 5–6

W
Wampi, 40, 73
Watering, 79–80
    avocado trees, 17
    banana plants, 21–22
    basin, 76, 79
    cherimoya trees, 25
    citrus trees, 30
    container plants, 90
    feijoa plants, 45
    fig trees, 47
    guava plants, 50
    and humidity, 9
    kiwi vines, 52
    litchi trees, 56
    loquat trees, 58
    macadamia trees, 60
    mango trees, 62
    methods of, 80
    papaya plants, 65
    passion vines, 67
    persimmon trees, 69
    tree tomato, 72
    white sapote, 71
White Sapote Crumb Squares, 72
Wind, 10

Z
Zapote blanco. *See* Sapote, white
Ziziphus jujuba, 75